THE RED HOT LUDGATE FAMILY

O
BOROUGH
OF
CHARD

LEON
Ingredients
& Recipes

Mmmm

Chill

LEON

Reading Borough Coun

D1333209

3412601050506 6

BOOK 2

LE○N

Naturally

FAST FOOD

By Henry Dimbleby & John Vincent

conran OCTOPUS

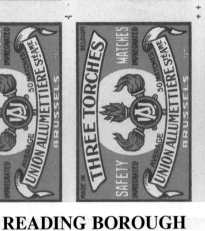

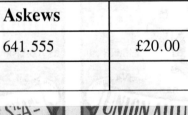

CONTENTS

John and Henry, December 2009

WELCOME TO
NATURALLY FAST FOOD

When we first started Leon, back in 2004, we tried to imagine what a high-street fast food joint might be like in heaven: a place where fresh, unprocessed, satisfying meals are served with pride. With the help of many people, especially Allegra and Benny, we have made some progress towards our long term goal of bringing the best food to the most people. In this book, we're hoping to bring some of that heaven home. We want to make it easy for everyone – whatever your level of culinary expertise – to eat well.

We've divided the book into two parts. The first section, Fast Food, is about dishes that can be conjured up in 20 minutes or less, from start to finish. The second section, Slow Fast Food, contains dishes that can be prepared in advance and then quickly reheated when you need them: think of them as your very own ready meals. There are also lots of bonus bits, but we'll let you find those.

This is not a book for the coffee table. It is a book we would like to be used, made messy, torn a little and stuck together with unidentified jammy bits.

Henry and John

A note on the authors

We have written this book in the first person plural – 'we' – because it is the fruit of our collective loins. It represents everything we – Henry and John, Allegra and all the other people who have helped build Leon – believe matters most about food.

In reality, of course, we all bring different things to the table. We've shared the writing of the general sections but when it comes to the recipes the way it works broadly speaking is this: Henry cooks and John eats.

Henry grew up in a foodie household (his mother is the cookery writer Josceline Dimbleby), and toyed with the idea of becoming a chef. After university he did a stint under the great Bruno Loubet, but concluded that he was too messy in the kitchen to make a career of it. Nevertheless, he knows cheffy things – how to chop things so fast you can't see the knife, for instance – and can knock up a feast for 20 without breaking a sweat. Food is his first love, and about two-thirds of the recipes in this book are his. But they would not have their distinctively Leon character without …

John – the eater. Although he makes a mean green chicken curry (see page 106), John is humble to the point of false modesty about his own cooking skills. 'The first time I offered to cook for my then-girlfriend, Katie,' he confesses, 'I turned up at her house with a jar of Chicken Tonight.' In the years since, Katie has made an honest man of him – and his taste in food has improved no end. John's interest in nutrition has been crucial in determining the Leon ethos. He believes that there are secrets out there that should not be secrets – such as the glycemic index, the damaging effects of sugar, good and bad fats, and the high incidence of wheat, gluten and dairy intolerance. John has a good palate and is invaluable at tastings. He is the people's representative at Leon, coming up with ideas for dishes that he thinks people will love, and making sure that the food keeps on tasting good and doing you good.

LOVE YOUR LARDER

Whether your larder is a whole room (lucky you) or just a couple of shelves, this is where you'll keep your arsenal of flavours.

These are our weapons of choice.

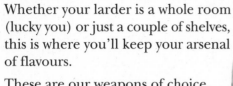

ANCHOVIES   CAPERS
Nature's flavour enhancers
(see page 128).

TOPPERS
Toasted, to give a little crisp finish to all sorts of dishes.
NUTS
Sliced almonds, cashews, hazelnuts, pine nuts.
SEEDS
Linseed, sunflower, pumpkin.

RUNNY HONEY
We use one made by bees that feed on orange blossom (this makes it naturally low GI – see page 294).

SPICES
Even in a small larder, it's worth going long on spices. They are the best way to bring a flavour hit to a quick dish. It is better if possible to buy cumin and coriander as whole seeds and grind them when you need them, as powders tend to go stale relatively quickly.

CARDAMOM PODS*
Warm, sweet, aromatic.

CORIANDER SEEDS*
Scented and lemony.

CUMIN*
Strong and meaty.

TURMERIC
Mild and warm.

CAYENNE
Hot.

SWEET PAPRIKA
Soft and smoky.

FENNEL SEEDS
For that aniseed kick.

* The curry triumvirate

DIJON MUSTARD

SOY

EXTRA VIRGIN OLIVE OIL
Ubiquitous now and rightly so. The healthiest and the tastiest oil. Worth spending some money to get a good one for dressings.

WHITE WINE VINEGAR
Colourless and therefore the most versatile of the vinegars.

CHICKEN STOCK CUBES

GOOD SEA SALT

BLACK PEPPERCORNS

THE CARBS

SPAGHETTI
The most versatile of the pastas (and if you cook it al dente it's low GI).

WHITE BASMATI
The easiest to cook and most versatile of the rices (lowish GI, too see page 294).

TINS

BARLEY COUSCOUS
The quickest carb of all, wheat-free and tastes every bit as good as the traditional couscous.

NUTMEG
For vegetable purées and anything dairy.

BEANS
For a simple stew, salad or side. Our favourites are flageolets, but chickpeas, butter beans, green lentils and cannellini beans all have their fans.

TOMATOES

Other things we keep to hand

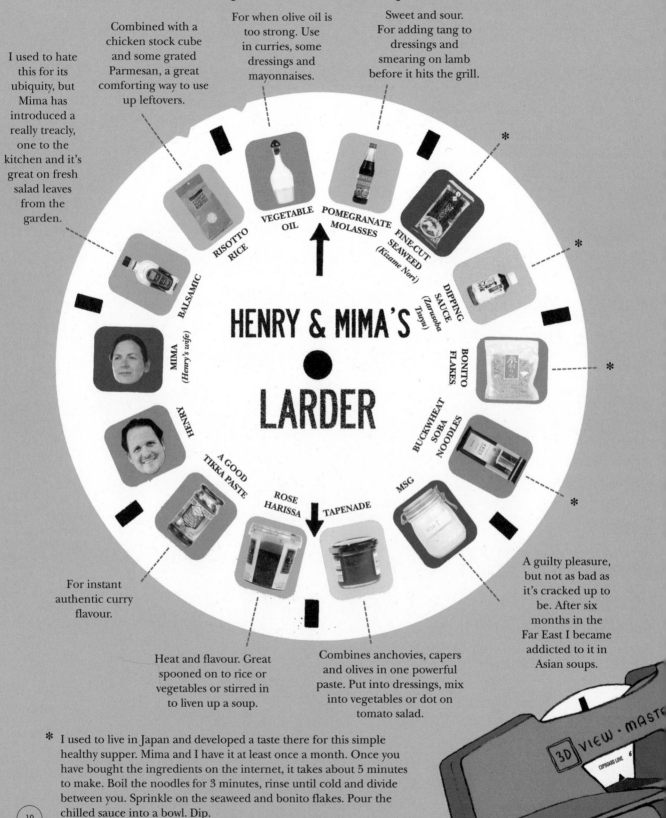

HENRY & MIMA'S LARDER

RISOTTO RICE — Combined with a chicken stock cube and some grated Parmesan, a great comforting way to use up leftovers.

VEGETABLE OIL — For when olive oil is too strong. Use in curries, some dressings and mayonnaises.

POMEGRANATE MOLASSES — Sweet and sour. For adding tang to dressings and smearing on lamb before it hits the grill.

FINE-CUT SEAWEED *(Kizame Nori)* *

DIPPING SAUCE *(Zarusoba Tsuyu)* *

BONITO FLAKES *

BUCKWHEAT SOBA NOODLES *

MSG — A guilty pleasure, but not as bad as it's cracked up to be. After six months in the Far East I became addicted to it in Asian soups.

TAPENADE — Combines anchovies, capers and olives in one powerful paste. Put into dressings, mix into vegetables or dot on tomato salad.

ROSE HARISSA — Heat and flavour. Great spooned on to rice or vegetables or stirred in to liven up a soup.

A GOOD TIKKA PASTE — For instant authentic curry flavour.

HENRY

MIMA *(Henry's wife)*

BALSAMIC — I used to hate this for its ubiquity, but Mima has introduced a really treacly, one to the kitchen and it's great on fresh salad leaves from the garden.

* I used to live in Japan and developed a taste there for this simple healthy supper. Mima and I have it at least once a month. Once you have bought the ingredients on the internet, it takes about 5 minutes to make. Boil the noodles for 3 minutes, rinse until cold and divide between you. Sprinkle on the seaweed and bonito flakes. Pour the chilled sauce into a bowl. Dip.

3D VIEW-MASTER

A good morning cleanse in hot water with lemon, and good on spelt toast for a healthy breakfast or snack. I've noticed that this is 50% cheaper in supermarkets than it is in health food shops.

One of the tastiest and, weirdly, healthiest fats one can cook with. Great for roast potatoes.

In honour of the Virgin Mary.

This sits right next to our cooker the whole time. It's the flavour cheat we add to rice to make it taste posh.

MANUKA HONEY

GOOSE FAT

LEE & PERRIN'S WORCESTER-SHIRE SAUCE

TABASCO

THAI CURRY PASTE

MARIGOLD SWISS VEGETABLE BOUILLON

JOHN & KATIE'S

KATIE (John's wife)

COCONUT MILK

LARDER

JOHN

BAMBOO SHOOTS

FISH SAUCE

DARK CHOCOLATE

RED CAMARGUE RICE

AGAVE SYRUP

* The key ingredients of the best thing in the culinary world, green chicken curry.

The cure for most of the world's problems. Big credit to our friends Dave and Sumi for eating our signature cabbage and chocolate dish.

I love the idea of an arable crop that is so specific to such a defined area, the product of the unique soil and climate. When Bambi Sloan (the Leon designer) comes to see us she cooks the greatest dishes with this. We try to replicate them when she has gone.

Very low GI, a natural sweetener that looks like it may be getting a better press than fructose right now.

LOVE YOUR FREEZER

The snobbery once associated with frozen food has disappeared, as people realize that freezing is a great way to preserve the vitamins and minerals in fruit and vegetables. A well-stocked freezer full of things you made earlier – soups, stews, chilli con carne, anything that suits reheating – is also a godsend on those nights when you just can't be bothered to cook. It'll stop you resorting to greasy takeaways, and therefore make you richer, thinner and happier.

In an ideal world we'd all have those vast American-style chest freezers – the kind you can store a corpse in, if you must. Instead, most of us make do with something rather smaller than the average television. It pays, therefore, to pack it judiciously. If you have a small freezer, don't bother filling it with raw meat or fish. You'll find it much more useful to have ready-cooked food to hand.

Our all-time freezer top ten would be:

(10) Toast (in the form of bread) Sliced bread freezes brilliantly, so you never need go short of a nice piece of grainy toast.

(9) Pastry Watch a basic casserole become a pie, as your friends look on admiringly.

(8) Vodka

(7) Frozen fruit & berries For instant smoothies. Try adding the vodka too.

(6) A stick of fresh horseradish Peeled and wrapped in clingfilm. Grate it from frozen and mix with yoghurt, mustard and vinegar for an instant fresh Sunday horseradish sauce.

(5) Home-made chicken stock Best in those little freezer bags as ice-cubes are too small and fiddly.

(4) Vanilla ice cream A good shop-bought one. (To dress it, see page 194.)

(3) Frozen peas Not just for putting on injuries after football … but because secretly they're everyone's favourite vegetable.

(2) Home-made soups, stews & leftovers Most of the dishes in the second half of this book are suitable for freezing. Double the quantities and freeze the rest. Freeze food in single portions – you don't want to have to defrost bolognese for ten when all you're after is a TV dinner for one. (Buy lots of small, resealable freezer bags, the sort where you can write the dish and date on the front.)

(1) Fish fingers The freezer king. You can buy really good chunky sustainable ones now. Cook from frozen to make the perfect fish finger butty.

GROW
YOUR
OWN

Painting by Elektra Mandy

GROW YOUR OWN

Mint   Oregano   Thyme   Chives (in season)

Nothing tastes quite as vibrant as food freshly pulled from the soil. And although growing your own vegetables can seem daunting, it really is true that anyone can do it – even if they don't have a square inch of garden to call their own.

In this section we hope to give everyone the confidence to grow something – whether on the windowsill, in the back garden or in a proper veg patch.

WHAT TO GROW *on your windowsill*

Even if the extent of your arable land is the ledge outside your kitchen, you can still be a farmer. Just with a slightly smaller harvest.

It's best to stick to herbs, which are easy to grow, expensive to buy and don't last long in the fridge. The herb flowers also look beautiful in salads.

Getting the right varieties is critical, as many garden centres sell plants that grow well but don't taste great.

Our four favourite windowbox herbs are:

Mint
Don't take this as a challenge, but it is almost impossible to kill mint. You can buy all sorts of fancy mints, but for our money you can't beat spearmint (*Mentha viridis*), also known as garden mint.

Oregano or marjoram
Greek oregano (*Origanum vulgare hirtum*) has a particularly good flavour and will thrive in a windowbox.

Thyme
There are some pretty flavourless varieties around, so be choosy. Have a little nibble on a leaf before you buy. Our favourite is the standard garden thyme (*Thymus vulgaris*).

Chives
Slice into salads and sauces for an oniony edge. Try *Allium schoenoprasum*, a specially bred compact variety well suited to windowboxes.

In addition to these four, sage and rosemary will grow very well in pots hanging off your walls. They are both pretty tolerant of drought, so it doesn't matter if you forget to water them. We particularly like purple sage (*Salvia officinalis purpurascens*), and you can't go wrong with *Rosmarinus officinalis*.

WHAT TO GROW *in your town garden*

Four years ago, Henry had an overwhelming urge to get up in the middle of the night, dig up half of his already small lawn and create a vegetable patch. These are his thoughts on the experiment.

In the days after I dug up our lawn, in a frenzy of good intentions – and possibly, subconsciously, to placate my wife, who had been fond of the lawn – I devised a detailed plan of crop rotation that would see our miniscule plot provide a third of our fruit and vegetables. And for a while I gave it a go: fixing nitrogen with beans, liming the suitcase-sized cabbage patch, and experimenting with American-style 'Three Sisters' planting patterns of corn, beans and squash.

George in the garden, age 1

It soon became clear, however, that with a smallholding as titchy as ours, it pays to concentrate on a few winning crops.

These days, I only plant things that:

a) can be grow in sufficient quantities in a small space to be used regularly, and b) taste much better than when you buy them in the shops. It is also fun to add some treats for children. So now we have a less adventurous garden – more Margo and Jerry than Barbara and Tom – but one that brings such a return on the minimal investment I make in it that it is my greatest pleasure.

With the help of my friend and fellow urban gardener Jojo Tulloh (author of *Freshly Picked: Kitchen Garden Cooking in the City*) I have put together a hit list of crops that are reliable, easy and tasty:

HERBS

Mint, Bay, Marjoram, Rosemary, Thyme, Oregano, Chives and Chervil	These are all easy to grow. Chervil is beautiful in salads.
Coriander, Basil, Parsley and Lovage	These are harder to grow. For the ambitious only.

COURGETTES

Nero di Milano	Lots of small glossy dark green fruits and a very nice open growing structure, which makes picking easy.
Sunburst	Productive and tasty, producing plump shiny yellow patty pan squash.

LETTUCE *a huge topic, as there are winter and summer crops. But here are some good ones:*

Thompson and Morgan's Saladisi	Buy a seed mixture if you don't know where to start.
Little Gem	You can't go wrong with this.
Rocket	Both wild (smaller spikier leaf) and the more fleshily-lobed cultivated version. Great in a salad bowl and peppery on pizzas and pasta.
Sorrel	Either French or buckler-leaved – is great cut into ribbons for a lemony zing in the salad bowl, or cooked with fish, or in soups, risotto and dhal. Jojo sees it as a total must, as it goes through the winter and self-seeds..
Catalogna	Also known as dandelion lettuce – has a great taste and a lovely undulating shape. It is slightly bitter, in a good way, and very productive.
Chinese mustard and golden mustard	Great for sowing in late summer and autumn to take you through the winter. They add a hot taste to salad, and work well as a bed for grilled meats (belly pork, chops, etc.); the leaves wilt slightly with the heat, and taste great dressed in the juices of the meat.

STRAWBERRIES

Alpine Strawberries	These go down well with children, who love to hunt for the tiny low-growing fruits. They like growing in pots, and look beautiful added to a fruit salad or scattered over yoghurt.

CUCUMBER

The Parisian Pickling variety	You can pick it small and pickle it for gherkins or let it grow big and eat as a cucumber.

TOMATOES

Shirley F1, Alicante	This varietal produces absurd amounts of insanely regular fruit with great taste.
Beefsteaks (e.g. Pink Brandy Wine)	These are less reliable, but amazing when they come off, with their soft, fondant, almost seedless interiors.
Plum tomatoes, San Marzano	A lovely flavour and delicately tapered fruits.
Cherry tomatoes (e.g. Gardener's Delight & Sungold)	Good and reliable.
Tiny Tim and Tumbling Tom	Perfect for hanging baskets, they are pretty and tasty.

WHAT TO GROW *in your country garden or allotment*

There are people better qualified than us in the art and science of planting, growing and harvesting vegetables, and luckily they have written some wonderful books. These are some of our favourites:

Katie enjoying the good life

Eleanor spotted carrying leeks

Natasha knows her onions

LOVE FOOD

If you are one of the people in these pictures, get in touch and you can eat free in Leon for a year. Photographs by Liam Bailey.

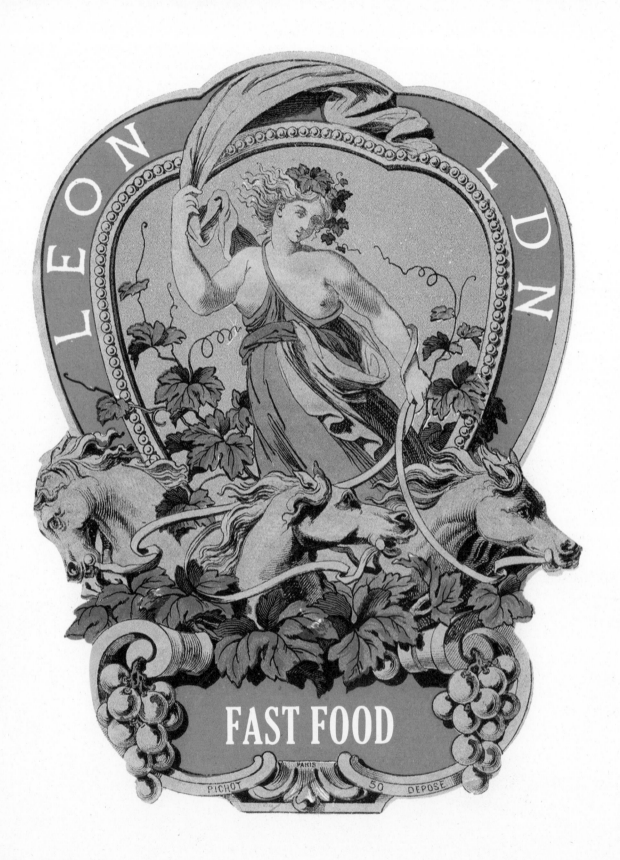

FAST FOOD

This section contains recipes that can be prepared in less than 20 minutes.

A few may require a little cooking time on top of that, but this is time you can use to finish a book, groom the cat, cuddle your partner, polish your shoes or catch up on a box set.

There is a guide at the top of each recipe to tell you exactly how much preparation time and cooking time we think it will take.*

Key to recipe icons (see page 294 for more details)

♥ = no or low animal fat

✓ = good carbs/good sugars

WF = wheat free

DF = dairy free

GF = gluten free

V = vegetarian

(🍴) = indulgence

*We have given times that we think are about right for the average amateur cook.
If you have wicked knife skills, you can probably slice off quite a few minutes.

Fast Food Tips

This book is, of course, one giant volume of fast food tips. But here we thought we'd share some particular techniques for speed and mastery in the kitchen.

SEASONING

This is the most important piece of advice in the book. Even when cooking quickly, take your time to season. Humdrum dishes can be transformed by the judicious application of salt, pepper, olive oil and lemon juice. Taste carefully. Add salt and pepper. Taste again. If the dish lacks body, add some oil (or a grating of Parmesan). If it lacks taste, a squeeze of lemon works wonders. Squeeze your lemon over a sieve to save having to pick out the pips – a time consuming and irritating task.

CHOPPING AND PEELING

Speedy chopping – without the visit to A&E. The trick is to get the tips of your fingers out of harm's way. Tuck them underneath your knuckles and away from the knife. Use your knuckles to guide the knife. You'll have the confidence to get slicing at speed.

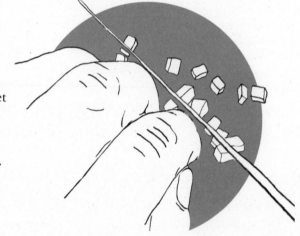

Stay sharp. Pick up a new or second-hand iron with which to sharpen your knives. You can get ones that look like this (diagram 1), or fancier contraptions with two rollers and a handle that look like this (diagram 2).

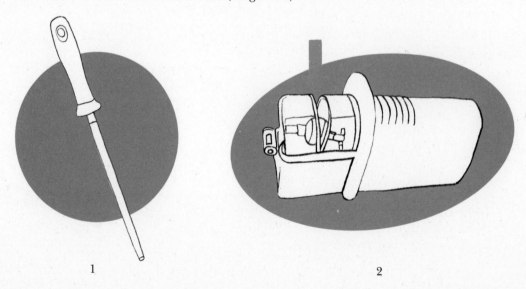

1

2

Invest in a great peeler. Otherwise, the ordeal of scraping away for hours can put you right off your root veg. The best ones are, of course, sharp, with a big gap between the two blades and a head that swivels easily – known as speed peelers.

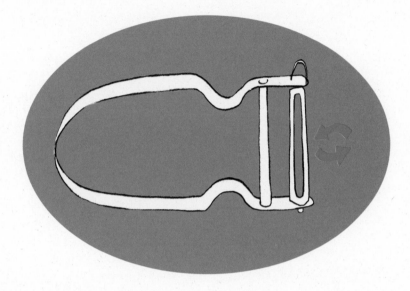

Peel ginger with a teaspoon. It saves time and waste.

COOKING

Minimize kitchen miles. So much time can be wasted walking from pillar to post when making food. Don't keep walking over to the bin: make a pile of waste. Keep the pans near the cooker, and ideally design your kitchen with the sink, fridge and cooker arranged in a triangle so that nothing is ever too far from reach.

Listen to music. Pop on your iPod and rev up the tempo. We don't actually know scientifically whether this makes you go faster, but it feels like it.

PREPARATION

Keep a good stock of Parmesan, onions and garlic. Almost any other ingredients can be made appetizing with these three must-keep-teers. (You can add lemons too if you miss d'Artagnan.)

Organize your cupboards. When you're in a hurry it can be infuriating trying to locate the measuring jug or weighing scales. So make sure everything has its place, as Grandma Edith used to say.

Take this book to work. You can read it on the way in, or on the way home. Or maybe at lunchtime. Or instead of looking at Facebook. That way you'll be able to start cooking the moment you get in.

RAPID BREAKFASTS

For Kurt Vonnegut, 'the breakfast of champions' was a martini. For Robert Burns it had to be porridge. According to Truman Capote, Marilyn Monroe knew how to eat it with gusto, while Audrey Hepburn did not.

BREAKFAST IS THE MOST IMPORTANT MEAL OF THE DAY

We are creatures of habit in the morning, but what all nutritional experts agree is that:

BREAKFAST IS THE MOST IMPORTANT MEAL OF THE DAY

It is also eaten when we are not at our most inspired and we don't have much time. To that end, here are a few ideas that might help you break out of a breakfast rut.

OMELETTES

For quick eggy breakfasts, omelettes are the way to go. Great scrambled eggs take too long, and poached eggs need company (see The Grill Up, page 32). An omelette, on the other hand, can be a full meal on a plate in under 5 minutes.

OMELETTE BAVEUSE: *The world's greatest omelette*

Discovering an omelette 'baveuse' is a game-changing moment in life. We were taught how to make them by our French friend Pierre. Many people leave the centre of the omelette a little moist or tacky like this, but there is a particular quality that can only come from cooking them at a low heat.

Pierre, Brighton 1925

FRIENDS & FAMILY RECIPES

Preparation time: 2 minutes
Cooking time: 2–3 minutes
✓ WF GF V

2 **eggs** per person
1 tablespoon grated **Cheddar cheese** per person
1 heaped spoonful of **crème fraîche** per person
a dash of **vegetable oil**
sea salt and **freshly ground black pepper**

1. Put the eggs, cheese, seasoning and crème fraîche into a bowl. Whip them up a little with a fork so that they are well mixed.

2. Get a non-stick pan reasonably hot and heat a dash of vegetable oil.

3. Pour in the egg mixture and tilt the pan so that it spreads around the base. With a wooden spatula, circle the edge of the pan and ensure that the edges remain loose. After 15 seconds reduce the heat to low.

4. When the top has a moist, tacky texture (see the photo), use the spatula to fold one side of the omelette over on to itself and slide it on to a plate. The omelette should be just coloured on the underside, and still slightly runny inside.

5. Eat immediately.

TIPS

RECIPE TESTED BY JOHN & HELEN

○ If you want to make the omelette a little healthier you can leave out the cheese and crème fraîche (or replace the crème fraîche with a little whole milk).

○ Great for a quick lunch or supper, served with crusty bread and lettuce salad.

The fillings Thirty seconds into cooking you can add a filling. We particularly like:

Healthy: Tomato and turmeric. Heat a little oil in a very hot pan. Roughly chop a tomato (1 per person) and add it to the smoking oil. Toss vigorously – some of the oil may well flare up, so don't do this in flammable pyjamas. Add a generous pinch of turmeric and season well. The tomatoes should still have shape but will be a bit saucy.

Classic & classy: Add fromage frais, smoked salmon and chives.

Cheesy: Add 50g more grated cheese per person, with chopped chives and parsley.

Mushroomy: Put Ultimate Mushrooms on Toast (page 110) inside the omelette instead.

Hammy: Prosciutto, crispy bacon or any other finely chopped cured meat.

THE GRILL UP *with easy poached eggs*

Like many good things in life, this is all about timing. Not a manic 3-Michelin-starred timing, but the right thing under the grill at the right time – so that you have time to make sure the coffee is just so.

Feeds: 2
Preparation time: 0 minutes
Cooking time: 20 minutes
✓ DF

2 **tomatoes**
2 large or 4 small flat, field or Portobello **mushrooms**
olive oil
2 free-range **eggs**
4 rashers of your favourite **bacon**
2 fat or 4 thin **pork sausages**
1 slice of **bread** per person – optional
sea salt and **freshly ground black pepper**

Minutes

1. Turn your grill on fairly high. Tear off a sheet of foil and put it shiny side down on a wide baking sheet. **0:00**

2. Cut your tomatoes and put them at one end in a row, followed by a neat row of whole mushrooms. Drizzle with a little olive oil and season well. Place the sausages on the tray as well. Pop the tray under the grill – on the highest shelf. **0:01**

3. Set up 2 teacups and tear off a piece of clingfilm for each one. Line the teacups and crack an egg into each. (If you are a confident egg poacher with super-fresh eggs, just do it your normal way at the end.) **0:03**

4. Put the bacon on the grilling tray and return it to the grill. Boil a kettle. **0:06**

   Bring up the edges of the clingfilm to a tight twist, leaving a little airspace next to the egg.

   Fill a small saucepan two-thirds full with boiling water, and put the pan on to boil.

5. Turn the sausages and bacon and pop back under the grill for another 5 minutes. **0:11**

6. If you like to have toast, get your bread either under the grill or in the toaster. **0:12**

   Gently drop your egg parcels into the boiling water in the pan, turn the heat down to a simmer and set your timer for 4 minutes for soft eggs or 5 for hard.

7. Assemble your brekkie on 2 plates. The eggs will be fine out of the water, in their clingfilm, for a minute or two. **0:16**

TIPS

○ Depending on the quality (and size) of your bacon and sausages, the time under the grill will wax or wane to get perfect crispy bacon or the best browned snags.

WONDERFUL YOGHURT

YOGHURT *with rose petal jam*

WF GF V

Fill a bowl with rich natural yoghurt and cover liberally with rose petal jam (available from Middle Eastern shops).

BREAKFAST BIRCHER

Makes: 150g
Preparation time: 12 hours
Cooking time: 0 minutes
♥ ✓ WF GF V

150g **oats**
400ml **apple juice**

1. In a large bowl, or Tupperware box, mix the oats with the apple juice, cover and leave overnight.

 TIPS ··

o Add flaxseeds, linseeds or any other seeds you may fancy. Soaking linseeds overnight helps them to release the Omega-3s.

o Fantastic eaten with natural yoghurt and masses of chopped fruit.

Tastes Good Does You Good

MINI KNICKERBOCKER GLORY

Makes: 2 glasses
Preparation time: 5 minutes
Cooking time: 0 minutes

♥ ✓ V

1 small **mango**
300g **natural yoghurt**
1–2 tablespoons **blackberry compote** (see page 260) or **jam**
1 tablespoon **honey**
80g **granola**

1. Peel and chop the mango into little cubes.

2. Take 2 clean medium-sized glasses and spoon a layer of yoghurt into the bottom of each one.

2. Top this with compote, followed by honey, and a further layer of yoghurt.

3. Scatter over some chopped mango, and finally top each glass with the granola.

TIPS

o   If you do not have compote or jam, use fresh berries.

A BREAKFASTY BANANA SPLIT

Feeds: 2
Preparation time: 5 minutes
Cooking time: 5 minutes

WF GF V

2 **bananas**
1 **apple**
40g **nuts** – cashews, hazelnuts, macadamias
10g **butter**
2 tablespoons **natural yoghurt**
1 tablespoon **runny honey**
2 tablespoons **Breakfast Bircher** (see page 35)

1. Peel the bananas and cut them in half lengthways.

2. Core and roughly chop up the apple. Toast the nuts over a medium heat in a dry frying pan, then remove and roughly chop.

2. Heat the butter in a thick-bottomed frying pan, add the honey and cook the bananas flat side down for 3 minutes, or until golden.

3. In a clean bowl mix together the yoghurt, the bircher, the chopped apple and the toasted nuts.

4. Place the bananas on your breakfast plate (2 halves each), and top with the yoghurt and nut mixture.

Above: Mini Knickerbocker Glory

Below: A Breakfasty Banana Split

What's a kale like you doing on a nice page like this?

QUICK SMOOTHIES & JUICES

The breakfast power smoothie has been a fixture on the Leon menu since we first opened on Carnaby Street. Like the sorcerer's apprentice, however, we are unable to resist the temptation to tinker. Here are some of our most successful experiments.

STRAWBERRY POWER SMOOTHIE

When we introduced this to our menu, one of our regulars described it as 'another small step for mankind'.

Makes: 2 medium glasses
Preparation time: 5 minutes
Cooking time: 0 minutes
✓ WF GF V

1 small **banana**
a small handful of fresh or frozen **strawberries**
60g **oats**
1 tablespoon **clear honey**
125ml **Greek yoghurt**
150ml **whole milk**

1. Peel the banana, and hull the strawberries.

2. Put all the ingredients into a smoothie machine or a blender and blitz together.

 TIPS

o If you can't get your hands on fresh or frozen strawberries, you can add strawberry jam.

BLACKBERRY POWER SMOOTHIE

We bring this on to the menu in autumn, when it's getting a little parky for strawberries.

Makes: 2 medium glasses
Preparation time: 5 minutes
Cooking time: 0 minutes
✓ WF GF V

1 small **banana**
a small handful of fresh or frozen **blackberries**
60g **oats**
1 tablespoon clear **honey**
125ml **Greek yoghurt**
150ml **whole milk**

1. Peel the banana, and pick over the blackberries.

2. Put all the ingredients into a smoothie machine or a food processor and blitz them together.

 TIPS

o If you can't get your hands on fresh or frozen blackberries, you can add blackberry jam.

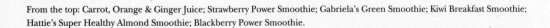

From the top: Carrot, Orange & Ginger Juice; Strawberry Power Smoothie; Gabriela's Green Smoothie; Kiwi Breakfast Smoothie; Hattie's Super Healthy Almond Smoothie; Blackberry Power Smoothie.

KIWI BREAKFAST SMOOTHIE

For those who don't fancy bananas, this smoothie makes a great substitute.

Makes: 4 medium glasses
Preparation time: 5 minutes
Cooking time: 0 minutes
♥ ✓ WF GF V

2 **kiwi fruits**
a large handful of **berries** of your choice
1 teaspoon **linseeds**
1 teaspoon **sunflower seeds**
125ml **Greek yoghurt**
125ml **fresh orange juice**

1. Peel the kiwis and wash the berries.

2. Put all the ingredients into a smoothie machine or a blender and blitz together until smooth.

HATTIE'S SUPER-HEALTHY ALMOND SMOOTHIE

And for those who are looking for something dairy free . . .

Makes: 2 medium glasses
Preparation time: 5 minutes
Cooking time: 0 minutes
♥ WF DF GF V

1 **kiwi fruit**
1 medium **banana**
2 large handfuls of **berries** – whatever is in season
8 **almonds**, skins on
2 heaped tablespoons **oats**
1 tablespoon **pumpkin seeds**
1 tablespoon **sunflower seeds**
250ml **rice milk**, **almond milk** or **soya milk**

1. Peel the kiwis and the banana. Wash the berries.

2. Put all the ingredients into a smoothie machine or a blender and blitz together until smooth.

Hattie, summer 2009

FRIENDS & FAMILY RECIPES

CARROT, ORANGE & GINGER JUICE

A great cold-buster, this has become a regular on the Leon menu.

Makes: 2 medium glasses
Preparation time: 5 minutes
Cooking time: 0 minutes
♥ ✓ WF DF GF V

3 **carrots**
a thumb-sized piece of **fresh ginger**
500ml freshly squeezed **orange juice**

1. Peel the carrots and the ginger.
2. Juice both in a juicing machine and pour into a large jug.
3. Add the freshly squeezed orange juice and mix well.

 TIPS

o If you only have a carton of orange juice, this is a great way to pep it up.

GABRIELA'S GREEN SMOOTHIE

Gabriela is a friend of ours who specializes in raw food (see page 152). This is not one for the faint-hearted. Some of us love it, for others it is inedible. It is made possible by the fact that raw kale is surprisingly sweet – try biting off a piece.

Makes: 6 glasses
Preparation time: 5 minutes
Cooking time: 0 minutes
♥ ✓ WF GF V

4 **kale** leaves, stalks removed
250ml **milk** or a dairy-free alternative,
    e.g. **rice milk, soya milk** or **nut milk**
1 **banana**
1 **pear**
1 tablespoon **honey**
1 tablespoon **almond butter**
1 level tablespoon **cocoa powder** (or, for
    raw food fanatics, **cacao powder**)

Gabriela preparing a feast, December 2009

1. Start by blending the kale with the milk and 150ml of water until there are no more chunks or bits.
2. Add the rest of the ingredients and blend well.

 TIPS

o If you can't find almond butter, use peanut butter.

FRIENDS & FAMILY RECIPES

PORRIDGE

Porridge is enjoying something of a comeback after years in the highland wilderness. Not only is it low GI, which means it keeps you feeling full for longer; it also magically lowers cholesterol levels. And best of all, it's a perfect vehicle for all sorts of scrumptious toppings. We serve bucketfuls of the stuff at Leon every day and are registered addicts.

BASIC PORRIDGE

To make porridge quickly, use rolled oats – not the pinhead ones, which take ages to cook. In the restaurants we make it with whole organic milk. At home we often make it with water – it depends how creamy you are feeling.

(Oats are gluten free, but have often been milled in a mill that also processes wheat. Be sure to check if this is important to you.)

Feeds: 2
Preparation time: 0 minutes
Cooking time: 5 minutes

♥ ✓ WF DF GF V

1 cup **rolled oats** (about 100g)
2 cups **water** (or **milk**, or a combination of the two)
salt

1. Put the oats, water and a good pinch of salt into a pan and cook over a medium heat for 4–5 minutes, stirring as you go.

2. Serve.

Classic porridge toppers

○ Cold milk with honey, a blob of jam, some dark muscovado sugar or golden syrup.

○ As above, but with Jersey double cream (Sundays only).

○ Banana rounds and honey (see opposite).

○ Crispy streaked bacon and maple syrup (a favourite with Daddy Bear – see opposite).

○ Fruity feast – an extravaganza of fresh fruit, compote, toasted nuts and seeds, and honey (see opposite).

Leon originals – favourites from the restaurants

○ Valrhona chocolate flakes

○ Banana, orange blossom honey and toasted seeds

○ Blackberry or strawberry compote

Opposite: Porridge topped with crispy bacon and maple syrup, a fruity feast and banana rounds and honey

When we were kids we would stay in Scotland for New Year. Every morning, porridge would be served from a huge bowl. Any leftovers would be poured into one of two 'porridge drawers' and left to set. The previous day's drawer would then be turned out and the porridge – all shiny and set – cut into bars for a long pre-lunch walk. They were surprisingly good.
Henry

TOPPED RYE BREAD

Of all the quick breakfasts, these are the quickest. Rye bread freezes well and toasts directly from frozen. It is wheat, and often yeast, free.

Most importantly, the modern rye breads no longer taste of Ukrainian footwear. They are soft and sweet and remarkably moreish.

What follows are ideas rather than recipes – we hope they will spark you into making some rye creations of your own.

New York Breakfast WF
The classic rye breakfast. Toast the rye. Smear on cream cheese. Top with smoked salmon, cucumber rings, chopped ripe tomatoes and finely sliced red onion. Squeeze over some lemon juice and sprinkle with chopped chives.

Cream Cheese & Blackcurrant Jam WF V
Think yoghurt and jam, but on an open sandwich.

Peanut Butter & White Grapes ♥ WF DF V
This is the healthy version of peanut butter and jello. Slice the grapes in half and either plonk them loosely on the peanut butter or arrange them in military rows for that classic '70s look.

Other rye toppers we love

The Continental	Like the New York breakfast, but substitute a good ham for the smoked salmon.
The Fruit & Nut	Any other combination of fruit and peanut butter. Fine slices of apple are particularly good.
Hot Berries	Heat honey, ground cinnamon and berries in a pan until the berries begin to lose their edges. Pop on to the rye and top with a blob of yoghurt.
The Wimbledon	Strawberries and banana tossed in a little thick yoghurt, with a touch of honey drizzled on top.
Honey & Banana Slices	Spread the honey on the rye and arrange the banana slices geometrically, just because it looks pretty.
The Full English	Sliced tomatoes (on the bottom), scrambled egg and a crispy slice of thin streaky bacon.
The Veggie English	Sliced tomatoes, topped with mushrooms that have been quick-fried in super-hot olive oil.
The Reichstag	Wholegrain mustard on the bottom, then sliced tomatoes, ham and finely sliced dill pickles. For extremists only.

From the top: New York Breakfast; Peanut Butter & White Grapes; Cream Cheese & Blackcurrant Jam

SATURDAY PANCAKES

For a luxurious – but wheat-free – start to Saturday morning.

Feeds: 4
Preparation time: 15 minutes
Cooking time: 15 minutes
♥ WF

3 **eggs**
125g **buckwheat flour**
1 large teaspoon **honey**
a big pinch of **baking powder**
140ml **organic milk**
sea salt

1. Separate the eggs. Place the yolks in a large bowl and add the buckwheat flour.

2. Add the honey, baking powder and a pinch of salt and mix thoroughly. Slowly add the milk to make a smooth batter. You can do all this the night before.

3. In a separate bowl, whisk the egg whites to firm peaks and fold gently into the yolk mixture.

4. Heat a non-stick pan, gently drop in spoonfuls of the mixture, and cook for 2–3 minutes on each side.

 TIPS

You can devise all sorts of toppings for your pancakes, but here are three of our favourites:

○   **Luxury:** caramelized apple and cream. Foam a blob of butter in a pan, toss in diced apples (1 apple per person), a sprinkling of cinnamon and a little sugar and fry till brown. Take off the heat and stir in some double cream at the end.

○   **Fruity:** blueberries, sliced banana and agave syrup.

○   **John's chocolate pancakes:** John will eat chocolate with almost anything. This makes a surprisingly good breakfast. Banana, grated dark chocolate (70 per cent cocoa solids) and agave syrup.

Saturday Pancakes with Caramelized Apple and Cream

QUICK SUPPERS & LUNCHES

VEG DISHES *Principles*

We have put our vegetable recipes near the front of the book because, increasingly, we regard veg as the main event of a good lunch or dinner. There are lots of reasons why: they are good for us; they put less pressure on the increasingly stressed stock of farming land; and of course, our mums told us to. But the best reason to eat your veg is that, done right, they can be so darn tasty.

Instead of making meat or fish the centrepiece of a feast, try serving three or four vibrant vegetable dishes with a small amount of flesh on the side – almost like a garnish.

Here are some general tips for making the most of your veg.

Tips for creating great vegetable dishes

Think colour: People start eating with their eyes, so think about how you can combine vegetables of different colours in one dish. In these pages you will find vibrant chilli on broccoli; the warm orange and reds of carrot and beetroot; green beans banded with sweet red tomatoes and golden garlic.

Think architecture: Shape and texture are critical to the way you taste. Stay that hand before it slices another carrot round! Try cutting them diagonally, in batons, into rough random shapes. Think about how the vegetables will look together and how they will feel in the mouth.

Think texture: There is a received wisdom currently – in our view misplaced – that one should cook all vegetables so they still have an audible crunch. Broccoli, green beans, runners and carrots will all absorb dressings and other flavours better if they are a little softer. Ripped vegetables have their place, but there is room for soft curves as well.

Think toppers: Something a little crispy on top makes vegetables a bit special. We like toasted nuts (flaked almonds, pine nuts, cashews, smashed hazelnuts), golden crisped garlic, crispy shallots, pan-toasted breadcrumbs, toasted seeds and Parmesan crusts.

Think flavour enhancers: Not MSG but the natural ones – olives, chilli, capers, anchovies, soy sauce, harissa. Don't be scared to give your vegetables a big flavour kick.

NATURAL FAST FOOD

Clockwise from the top: Roast Crispy Cauliflower with Turmeric; Carrots & Beetroot with Toasted Almonds; Purple Sprouting Broccoli with Flageolets & Hazelnuts

ROAST CRISPY CAULIFLOWER *with turmeric*

Simple and very moreish – great with beer or as a side.

Feeds: 4
Preparation time: 3 minutes
Cooking time: 30 minutes
♥ ✓ WF DF GF V

1 **cauliflower**
4 tablespoons **extra virgin olive oil**
1 teaspoon **turmeric**
1 teaspoon **black onion seeds**
sea salt and **freshly ground black pepper**

1. Preheat the oven to 200°C/400°F/gas mark 6.

2. Cut the cauliflower into thumb-sized florets, discarding the stalk, and put into a roasting tray. Add the oil, turmeric, onion seeds, salt and pepper and toss. Spread out evenly in the tray.

3. Put into the oven for 30 minutes, shuffling the tray once after 15 minutes.

 **TIPS**

○ You can use a curry or tikka paste from a jar instead of turmeric.

○ The smaller florets can get a bit burnt, but that can be nice.

○ Good with feta crumbled over the top and served with a salad for a simple supper.

○ Fred loves it with yoghurt, mixed with chilli and lime juice.

CARROTS & BEETROOTS *with toasted almonds*

Beautiful to look at and extremely straightforward to make (pictured on page 51).

Feeds: 4 (with room to spare)
Preparation time: 5 minutes
Cooking time: 45 minutes
♥ ✓ WF DF GF V

750g whole raw **beetroots**
750g **carrots**
4 tablespoons **extra virgin olive oil**
1½ tablespoons **runny honey**
1 tablespoon **balsamic vinegar**
80g **flaked almonds**
3 tablespoons **fresh chervil** or **parsley leaves** – optional
sea salt and **freshly ground black pepper**

1. Preheat the oven to 200°C/400°F/gas mark 6.

2. Peel the beetroots and cut them into substantial chunks. Peel the carrots and cut them into batons.

3. Put the beetroots and carrots into separate oven dishes, coat with olive oil and season well with salt and pepper. Add the honey to the carrots and the balsamic to the beetroot and stir well.

4. Put both trays into the oven for 45 minutes, or until the carrots are starting to brown and the beetroots are soft.

5. Meanwhile, dry-toast the almonds in a frying pan over a medium heat on the hob, being careful not to burn them. Chop the parsley, if using.

6. Place the cooked vegetables on a serving dish. Scatter over the chervil or parsley and the almonds.

 TIPS ....

- This would go well with natural yoghurt or some hummus and warm bread.

PURPLE SPROUTING BROCCOLI *with flageolets & hazelnuts*

With the beans adding protein, this makes a great stand-alone supper; the red onion adds sweetness, the nuts give crunch. Make sure you cook the broccoli till it is soft enough to soak up all the savoury flavours (pictured on page 51).

Feeds: 4 as a side, 2 as a main
Preparation time: 10 minutes
Cooking time: 15 minutes
♥ ✓ WF DF GF

500g **purple sprouting broccoli**
50g whole peeled **hazelnuts**
4 cloves of **garlic**
25g **anchovies** (½ a tin)
6 tablespoons **extra virgin olive oil**
200g **red onions**
1 x 400g tin of **flageolet beans**, drained
½ a **lemon**
sea salt and **freshly ground black pepper**

1. Put a pan of salted water on to boil. Trim off the woody stalks from the broccoli. Break up the hazelnuts by placing in a clean tea towel and bashing with a rolling pin, or roughly chop them in a food processor. Toast the hazelnuts in a dry pan over a high heat, and set aside.

2. Peel and roughly chop the garlic. Chop the anchovies. Heat the olive oil in a non-stick frying pan, add the garlic and cook for a minute. Peel and chop the onions into semi circles, and add them to the garlic along with the anchovies.

3. Toss the onions over a high heat for 2 minutes. Turn the heat down to medium and cook for a further 5–10 minutes, or until the onions are soft. Season well with salt and pepper then add the beans, allowing them to just heat through.

4. Blanch the broccoli in the boiling water for 4 minutes (we like it a bit on the well cooked side for this dish), and drain. Arrange the broccoli on a big plate and scatter over the bean and onion mix. Squeeze over the juice of half a lemon and sprinkle the toasted hazelnuts on top before serving.

 TIPS ....

- You can use many other green vegetables as the base – broccoli, kale, runner beans or green beans would all work. If you use everyday broccoli, just slice off the woody end and use the peeled stalk as well as the florets. Waste not, want not.

- You can substitute any type of bean for the flageolets.

- For vegetarians, use capers instead of anchovies.

JOSSY'S BURMESE SPICY CABBAGE

All over Burma you find variations of both cabbage and cauliflower served in this way, with lots of health-giving turmeric and ginger – great on rice or as a side dish.

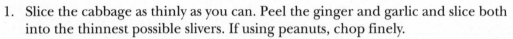

Jossy on the beach in Lanzarote, 1973

Feeds: 4 (as a side dish)
Preparation time: 15 minutes
Cooking time: 7 minutes

♥ ✓ WF DF GF

400g **green cabbage**
2.5cm piece of **fresh ginger**
3 large cloves of **garlic**
75g roasted unsalted **peanuts** – optional
1 level teaspoon **turmeric**
juice of ½ a **lemon**
1 tablespoon **fish sauce**
2 tablespoons **peanut oil**
a large handful of **fresh coriander leaves**,
     roughly chopped

I first tasted a dish like this at a stall on a Rangoon street in 1981.
Jossy

1. Slice the cabbage as thinly as you can. Peel the ginger and garlic and slice both into the thinnest possible slivers. If using peanuts, chop finely.

2. Pour 100ml of hot water into a measuring jug, add the turmeric and stir until smooth, then add the lemon juice and fish sauce.

3. Heat the peanut oil in a wok over a medium heat, then add the sliced cabbage and stir for a minute or two, or until it just begins to soften.

4. Now add the slivers of ginger and garlic, and the chopped peanuts and continue stirring around for another 2–3 minutes.

5. Pour in the turmeric liquid. Stir over the heat for another minute or so, and throw in the coriander leaves just before serving.

TIPS

o Add another squeeze of lemon juice if you feel it needs an extra lift once you have tasted it.

o A teaspoon of chilli powder and some sesame seeds also make good additions.

o It is a good dish to eat on its own with some rice or other vegetables, but would also be nice with some very simple grilled chicken.

Some words about Jossy by Henry

Being the offspring of a cookery writer is a privilege. I didn't learn to cook at Mum's elbow – she was always busy making notes and would shoo me and my sisters out of the kitchen. But I learned to eat. Meal after meal we were the guinea pigs for experiments with new dishes that she had picked up at home and abroad. (The stepdaughter of a diplomat, she was brought up in Syria and Peru and never lost her touch with spices.)

When John, Allegra and I opened Leon she would be there several times a week, tasting, making notes and giving advice. And again with this book she has been invaluable, testing recipes and suggesting ideas. She even offered some fast recipes of her own.

So if you see a recipe with this mark, *Jossy* you will know it is one of hers.
Thanks Mum.

MAIL
ION

FRIENDS & FAMILY RECIPES

ITALIAN BROAD BEANS

An easy and delicious storecupboard dish. Serve it either hot with grilled chicken, fish or meat, or as part of a cold meal, dribbled with olive oil.

Feeds: 4 (as a side)
Preparation time: 5 minutes
Cooking time: 15 minutes
♥ ✓ WF DF GF V

2–3 large cloves of **garlic**
1 x 400g tin of **chopped tomatoes**
2 tablespoons **extra virgin olive oil**
350g frozen **broad beans**
a small handful of fresh **basil leaves**
sea salt and **freshly ground black pepper**

1. Peel the garlic and slice into very thin slivers.

2. Put the tomatoes, garlic and olive oil into a heavy saucepan and season generously with salt and black pepper.

3. Bring up to bubbling point and add the broad beans.

4. Bring the mixture to the boil again, then reduce the heat and simmer gently in the open pan for 10–15 minutes, or until the sauce has reduced and any liquid has evaporated.

5. Add the basil leaves, check the seasoning and serve.

 TIPS

○ For extra depth of flavour, fry a finely chopped rasher of bacon or a couple of anchovies in the pan at the start, before you add the tomatoes.

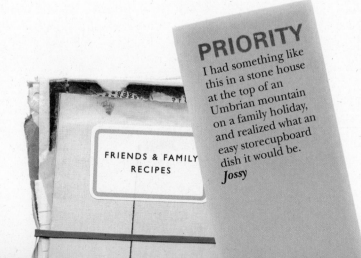

> **PRIORITY**
> I had something like this in a stone house at the top of an Umbrian mountain on a family holiday, and realized what an easy storecupboard dish it would be.
> *Jossy*

FRIENDS & FAMILY RECIPES

From the top: Italian Broad Beans; Carrot Purée;
Flash-fried Courgettes with Green Sauce

CARROT PURÉE

Good comfort food, and excellent with roast chicken; it tastes astonishingly good for something so simple (pictured on page 56).

Feeds: 4 (as a side dish)
Preparation time: 10 minutes
Cooking time: 30 minutes
✓ WF GF V

800g **carrots**
30g **butter**
1 whole **nutmeg**
sea salt and **freshly ground black pepper**

1. Put a pan of salted water on the hob to boil.

2. Cut the carrots into large chunks, put them into the pan and cook for 30 minutes, or until soft.

3. Drain the carrots and leave in a colander for 2 minutes to dry out.

4. Put them into a food processor, add the butter and whizz until completely smooth.

5. Grate in nutmeg to taste. Season.

 TIPS

○ Make sure the carrots are properly cooked and soft, otherwise they won't blend to a smooth consistency.

○ This purée is particularly good with simple grilled lamb chops.

○ If you want to be healthy you can use olive oil in place of the butter. If you want to be super-luxurious you can add more butter and some cream.

○ You can purée almost any vegetable with butter and nutmeg like this to great effect. Particularly good are parsnips or celeriac with game or beef, and Brussels sprouts, which you can purée in advance to save time on Christmas Day.

FLASH-FRIED COURGETTES *with green sauce*

Feeds: 4
Preparation time: 5 minutes
Cooking time: 5 minutes
♥ ✓ WF DF GF

700g **courgettes**
3 cloves of **garlic**
4 tablespoons **extra virgin olive oil**
sea salt and **freshly ground black pepper**
a drizzle of **Green Sauce** (recipe on page 141)

1. Slice the courgettes on the diagonal about 1cm thick. Finely chop the garlic.

2. Heat the oil in a large heavy-bottomed frying pan. Add the courgettes and cook fast until they start to brown (about 4 minutes). Add the garlic a minute before serving. Toss vigorously. Season well.

3. Serve immediately and drizzle with Green Sauce (see picture on page 56).

JOHN'S BROCCOLI *with garlic, cashew nuts & chilli*

Feeds: 4
Preparation time: 5 minutes
Cooking time: 10 minutes
♥ ✓ WF DF GF V

500g **broccoli**
3 cloves of **garlic**
2 fresh **red chillies**
2 tablespoons **rapeseed oil** or
   groundnut oil
a small handful of **cashews**
a hearty splash of **light soya sauce**
1 **lime**, cut into quarters

1. Cut the broccoli into medium-sized florets and steam them lightly over boiling water so that they are partly cooked.

2. Peel and finely slice the garlic and chillies. Put them into a large frying pan over a medium heat with the rapeseed or groundnut oil and fry until starting to soften.

3. Add the cashews and broccoli and stir well, so that everything is coated with oil and golden garlic.

4. Add the soya sauce, cover with a lid and cook for a further 2 minutes.

5. Finish with a squeeze of lime.

 TIPS

○ This can be turned into a more substantial dish for 4 people by adding 2 fillets of salmon.

IMMEDIATE I cooked this dish (with the salmon) a few months ago when I was in need of a quick lunch, and used pretty much everything I had in the kitchen at the time. I sat back to eat it at my desk and really enjoyed the next ten minutes of eating pleasure. The combination of chillies, soy sauce and cashews helped make this very healthy dish a triumph of flavour. Simple and speedy.
John

JOANNA'S PURPLE SPROUTING BROCCOLI
with sausage, chilli & fennel

Feeds: 4
Preparation time: 10 minutes
Cooking time: 20 minutes
✓ WF DF (GF if the sausages are GF)

Our friend Joanna Weinburg taught us how to make this. Supper or lunch in just one bowl, with a surprising depth of flavour for such a simple dish.

4 cloves of **garlic**
1 tablespoon **extra virgin olive oil**
½ teaspoon **dried chilli flakes**
2 teaspoons **fennel seeds**
800g plain best-quality **pork sausage meat**
(or sausages, squeezed out of their skins)
800g **purple sprouting broccoli**
juice of 1 **lemon**

1. Peel and roughly chop the garlic, then heat the oil in a frying pan and gently fry the chilli, garlic and fennel seeds until the garlic is golden.

2. Crumble in the sausage meat, turning it well in the mixture and breaking it up. Fry until the bottom becomes golden, then turn and break up again.

3. Chop the broccoli roughly and add to the pan. Turn well to coat it in the oil. Partly cover the dish and leave to cook for 5–7 minutes. The broccoli will still be crunchy.

4. Stir again, squeeze over the lemon juice, divide between plates and eat immediately.

TIPS

- It works beautifully with purple sprouting broccoli, but you could try it with kale, too.

- The key is to use a large pan so you have plenty of room to break up the sausage meat and brown it. If the pan is too crowded, it will steam instead, and steamed sausage meat will not make anyone happy. Use sausage with a high meat content. Great served with crusty bread, preferably sourdough.

I first ate this dish in New York when I was living in a tiny apartment with no natural light (as you do), above the extractor fan of an Italian restaurant (as you do) called Il Bagatto on the Lower East Side. They made a version of this dish with *broccoli di rape*, a wonderfully bitter green that is quite difficult to find. It takes me right back to the exciting hum of Manhattan living. **Joanna**

Joanna Weinberg, 1974"

FRIENDS & FAMILY
RECIPES

FRED'S ASPARAGUS

A very simple way with asparagus.

Feeds: 4
Preparation time: 5 minutes
Cooking time: 5–10 minutes

♥ ✓ WF DF GF V

600g **asparagus**
a medium handful of **fresh parsley**
a medium handful of **fresh tarragon**
2 tablespoons **extra virgin olive oil**
sea salt and **freshly ground black pepper**

*Fred and his friend
Andy Weller, 2010*

1. Snap the root ends off the asparagus and rinse well.

2. Place the whole asparagus spears on a griddle or frying pan, and cook for 5–10 minutes over a low heat. There is no need to add any water or oil.

2. Meanwhile, chop the parsley and tarragon finely, and mix together in a bowl with the olive oil, salt and pepper.

3. Plate up your cooked asparagus, drizzle with the herb oil and serve.

FRIENDS & FAMI
RECIPES

My brother Fred is almost 30 years younger than me and something of a carnivore. He likes to spend his Friday evenings lamping on the downs for rabbits with his friends. He makes a mean rabbit stew. This is him in more vegetarian mode.
Henry

RUNNER BEANS *with tapenade, tomatoes & golden garlic*

Perfect as part of a veggie dinner, or as a summer side with lamb, chicken or fish.

Feeds: 6 (as a side dish)
Preparation time: 15 minutes
Cooking time: 15 minutes

♥ ✓ WF DF GF

(V if you use anchovy-free tapenade)

5 cloves of **garlic**
6 tablespoons **extra virgin olive oil**
500g **runner beans**
350g **tomatoes** (about 3 medium ones)
4 level teaspoons **tapenade**
sea salt and **freshly ground black pepper**

1. Fill a pan with salted water and bring it to the boil.

2. Peel the garlic and chop roughly. Heat 2 tablespoons of olive oil in a pan on a medium heat. Cook the garlic until golden and pour into a small dish.

3. Cut the ends off the runner beans, cut them on the diagonal into long diamonds and add them to the boiling water. Cook until tender, drain, then dress with 2 tablespoons of olive oil and 2 teaspoons of tapenade. Season and spread on a plate.

4. Heat 2 tablespoons of olive oil in a very hot frying pan. Roughly chop the tomatoes into 1cm cubes and throw them in. Season with salt, pepper and the remaining 2 teaspoons of tapenade. Cook vigorously for a couple of minutes until softened.

5. Heap the tomato and tapenade mixture into the centre of the beans, scatter over the golden garlic and serve.

TIPS

○ Don't worry about cooking the beans too crisp. Softer veg absorb more flavour.

○ You can substitute almost any type of greens for the runner beans.

Above: Runner Beans with Tapenade, Tomatoes & Golden Garlic; Below: Fred's Asparagus with Herb Oil

Hoppy's LEEKS VINAIGRETTE

Leeks vinaigrette is a classic vegetable dish, and Simon Hopkinson does it best – the vinaigrette itself is unsurpassed. This is an adaptation of his recipe.

Feeds: 4
Preparation time: 10 minutes
Cooking time: 15 minutes

♥ ✓ WF DF GF V

1.5kg **leeks** (about 8 medium)
1 tablespoon **Dijon mustard**
1 tablespoon **red wine vinegar**
150ml **groundnut oil** or other flavourless oil
1 tablespoon **chopped fresh chives**
2 tablespoons **capers**
sea salt and **freshly ground black pepper**

1. Trim the leeks, split each one down the middle lengthwise (leaving the base on to keep the two halves together), and wash thoroughly in warm water to remove any dirt.

2. Bring a large saucepan of salted water to the boil. Add the leeks and cook them for around 15 minutes, or until they are tender.

3. Put the mustard, vinegar and 2 tablespoons of water into a blender or food processor and blend. With the machine still running, gradually add the oil until all the ingredients are homogenized. Season with salt and pepper. Add a little water if you think the dressing is too thick.

4. Drain the leeks well in a colander. Allow to cool a little, then cut off the base so that they separate into halves. Arrange neatly in a serving dish, cut sides downwards. Drizzle with the dressing.

5. Chop the capers and sprinkle over the leeks, together with the chopped chives.

TIPS

o It is essential that you don't use olive oil for this dish. As Simon says: 'The dressing is important – and a good one too, if I might say – as it not only doesn't use olive oil, but is all the better for it being omitted from a salad dressing, for once; oh! the ubiquity of that particular lotion, these days, delicious as it surely is…'

o Simon serves his leeks with a chopped hard-boiled egg on top instead of capers.

o Parsley can be used instead of chives.

o This can be made well in advance. It gets better as the vinaigrette seeps into the leeks. If you serve it from the fridge, make sure you let it warm up for an hour or so at room temperature, as cold food doesn't taste of much.

o This is great as a light dinner, with some sourdough toast and a poached egg.

Simon has been an inspiration to me from a young age. He is a chef who loves eating (not as common as it might seem). A wholesome greediness and a generosity of spirit permeate his books. The food is simple but – as he proves with this vinaigrette – he always gets the proportions just right to create something sensational.
Henry

FRIENDS & FAMILY
RECIPES

ROASTED VEG TIPS

The Ford Mondeo of roasted vegetable dishes – generally picked up during student days – usually involves chopping a random selection of vegetables into chunks of military regularity and throwing them into a roasting pan with some oil, salt and pepper. Back then, if we were feeling flamboyant, we might add some fluffy dice or a beaded seat-cover in the form of vinegar or a sprig of rosemary. And very nice they were too, thank you very much. With a little more care, however, it is possible to create something quite sophisticated. Here's how:

- **Choose your ingredients wisely.** Don't just throw in everything you have to hand. Two or three vegetables that go well together will be much more satisfying. Likewise, think about what herb or spice will add that perfect burst of flavour rather than reaching for the rosemary every time.

- **Think about the look as well as the taste.** We eat first with our eyes, and cutting vegetables elegantly makes them more alluring. It can also affect the flavour – cutting parsnips thinly, for example, ensures maximum golden gooeyness.

- **Play with texture.** Whether it is crunch in the form of nuts, or a crispy topping of Parmesan and breadcrumbs, a little texture lifts the dish to the next level.

ROAST PARSNIPS & CARROTS *with honey & fennel seeds*

The carrots and parsnips in this recipe are cut into long strips so they go nice and golden in colour.

Feeds: 4
Preparation time: 10 minutes
Cooking time: 40 minutes

♥ ✓ WF DF GF V

600g **carrots**
600g **parsnips**
2 heaped tablespoons **runny honey**
2 tablespoons **olive oil**
2 teaspoons **fennel seeds**
sea salt and **freshly ground black pepper**

1. Preheat the oven to 190°C/375°F/gas mark 5.

2. Chop the carrots and parsnips into long elegant strips and put into a large roasting tray.

3. Add the honey, oil, fennel seeds and seasoning, and mix together roughly with your hands.

4. Cook in the oven for 40 minutes, or until tender and golden.

TIPS

- Some whole cloves of garlic make a good addition.

Clockwise from the top: Roast Carrots & Fennel in Parmesan Breadcrumbs; Mediterranean Roast Vegetables; Parsnips & Carrots with Honey & Fennel Seeds

MEDITERRANEAN ROAST VEGETABLES

Summery roast vegetables, served with green sauce and great with grilled meat or fish (pictured on page 67).

Feeds: 4 (as a side)
Preparation time: 5 minutes
Cooking time: 45 minutes

♥ ✓ WF DF GF V

2 small **aubergines**, or 1 large
2 **courgettes**
200g **cherry tomatoes**
6 tablespoons **olive oil**
2 tablespoons **white wine vinegar**
70g **pine nuts**
sea salt and **freshly ground black pepper**

1. Preheat the oven to 200°C/400°F/gas mark 6.

2. Cut the ends off the aubergines and slice them thinly lengthways, from top to bottom. Cut the courgettes into batons, and halve the tomatoes.

3. Put the aubergines into an oven dish and scatter the courgettes and tomatoes over the top.

4. Sprinkle with the olive oil and vinegar, and season with salt and pepper. Place the dish in the oven to cook for 45 minutes.

5. Scatter the pine nuts over the vegetables 5 minutes before you are ready to take them out of the oven, so that they can brown. Be careful they don't burn.

6. Drizzle over a few spoonfuls of Green Sauce (page 141) and serve.

TIPS

○ Cooking times may vary a little depending on the kind of dish or oven pan you are using, so use a little common sense to prevent the vegetables either burning, or being undercooked, which is always unpleasant when eating aubergines.

Souvenir from Mallorca, 1976

ROAST CARROTS & FENNEL *in Parmesan breadcrumbs*

A crisp and scented alternative to traditional roast vegetables (pictured on page 67).

Feeds: 4
Preparation time: 15 minutes
Cooking time: 35 minutes

♥ ✓ V

500g **carrots**
500g **fennel**
a large bunch of **fresh rosemary**
4 tablespoons **extra virgin olive oil**
80–100g **stale white bread**
3 cloves of **garlic**
40g grated **Parmesan cheese**
sea salt and **freshly ground black pepper**

1. Preheat your oven as high as it will go.

2. Peel the carrots and cut into 1cm diagonal discs. Trim the fennel and cut into long elegant wedges (each bulb in half, then into 8–10 slices depending on thickness). Pick the leaves off the rosemary.

3. Put the vegetables into a large roasting tray. Add the olive oil and 100ml of water. Place on the top shelf of the oven for 20 minutes, turning after 10 minutes.

4. Put the bread, rosemary leaves, garlic, salt and pepper into the blender, and blitz until fine.

5. Once the carrots and fennel are cooked (the carrots should have some bite and the fennel should be translucent), sprinkle over the breadcrumb mix and top with the Parmesan.

6. Put back into the oven for a further 15 minutes.

TIPS

- If you don't have any breadcrumbs, you can use fine couscous instead. Simply scatter it over the vegetables, sprinkle with the finely grated Parmesan, and roast as usual.

- You can make stale bread by putting small chunks of fresh bread into the oven for 10 minutes at 110°C/225°F/gas mark ¼.

- Use a micrograter to grate the Parmesan for an extra fine and crunchy topping.

QUICK SOUPS

Gandhi said, 'Drink your food and chew your drink.' He might have been on to something. Lots of recent studies have shown that eating soup is a quick route to svelte thighs and a small but healthy tummy.

In our restaurants, the soups change every day and reflect the seasons. This gives us lots of opportunity for being adventurous with new dishes. Some of the soups in this section are from the restaurants, others are from our family recipe books.

JERUSALEM ARTICHOKE SOUP

Feeds: 4
Preparation time: 25 minutes
Cooking time: 55 minutes

✓ WF GF

1kg **Jerusalem artichokes**
lemon juice
1 large **onion**
25g **butter**
1 litre **whole milk**
1 **chicken stock cube**
1 tablespoon **chopped fresh flat-leaf parsley**
sea salt and **freshly ground black pepper**

1. Peel and chop the artichokes, and leave them in a pan of water with a squeeze of lemon juice to stop them going brown.

2. Peel and chop the onion.

3. Heat the butter in a pan and sauté the onion and artichokes until soft, but not brown.

4. Add the milk and crumble in the stock cube. Stir well and simmer for 35–45 minutes.

5. When cool enough, blitz in a blender until smooth and reheat to serve.

6. Season with salt and pepper and sprinkle with the parsley. You could add a swirl of double cream if you wish, too.

Leon (right) in the RAF, Cyprus 1958

COURGETTE SOUP

This soup is equally good hot or cold, depending on the season.

Feeds: 4
Preparation time: 5 minutes
Cooking time: 40 minutes
♥ ✓ WF GF

550g **courgettes**
1 large **onion**
30g **butter**
750ml **chicken stock**
sea salt and **freshly ground black pepper**

1. Trim and slice the courgettes. Finely chop the onion.

2. Melt the butter in a large saucepan. Add the onion and sauté gently for about 5 minutes, or until soft but not brown.

3. Add the courgettes, stir for a minute, then add the stock and bring to the boil. Cover and simmer gently for 30 minutes.

4. Whizz with a hand blender or in a food processor and season with salt and pepper to taste. Serve hot, or cold from the fridge in summer.

FRIENDS & FAMILY RECIPES

My grandmother made the most delicious soups, despite lacking the patience to make real stock. In 1994, she wrote out all her recipes for me by hand. There was, she assured me, no need to go hunting around for 'nonsensical sprigs of unobtainable herbs': a Knorr chicken stock cube and a handful of veg ('preferably fresh') was all anyone needed for a feast.
Mima

Mima and Hattie with their parents and grandparents, 1977

Courgette Soup (above) and
Jerusalem Artichoke Soup

JOSSY'S MYSTERY SOUP

So called because nobody ever guesses what this creamy pale green soup is made from, and though you may think the combination of ingredients sounds doubtful, it's delicious, and good hot or chilled.

Feeds: 4 as a main, 6 as a starter
Preparation time: 5 minutes
Cooking time: 15 minutes

✓ WF GF

450g thin **leeks**
2 **chicken stock cubes**
1 large ripe **avocado**
juice of ½ a small **lemon**
150ml **double cream**
a large handful of **fresh flat-leaf parsley**
sea salt and **cayenne pepper**

1. Prepare the leeks and slice across them finely, using as much of the green part as possible.

2. Pour 1.2 litres of water into a pan, crumble in the stock cubes, and stir over a medium heat until dissolved. Bring to the boil, add the sliced leeks, cover the pan and simmer for 8–10 minutes, or until the leeks are soft.

3. Meanwhile, cut the avocado in half, scoop out the flesh and put it into a food processor with the lemon juice and cream. Whizz until very smooth. Chop the parsley very finely.

4. Add the avocado purée to the leeks and stir to mix evenly.

5. Bring the soup to the boil again for just a minute, then stir in the chopped parsley and remove from the heat.

6. Season with salt and cayenne pepper.

 TIPS

○ If you're not intending to eat it at once and need to reheat the soup later, remove it from the heat immediately it begins to bubble.

From the top: Mystery Soup; Butter Bean Soup with Grilled Peppers & Sautéed Garlic; Belinda's Chicken Noodle Soup

BUTTER BEAN SOUP *with grilled peppers & sautéed garlic*

Butter beans make a wonderfully smooth and soothing soup, but this one has great kick and texture too (pictured on page 75).

Feeds: 4–5
Preparation time: 15 minutes
Cooking time: 10 minutes

✓ WF GF V

1 large **red pepper**
2 x 400g tins of **butter beans**
75g unsalted **butter**
600ml **whole milk**
4 large cloves of **garlic**
2 tablespoons **olive oil**
2–4 pinches of **chilli powder** or **dried chilli flakes**
juice of 1 **lemon**
sea salt

1. Quarter the pepper lengthways and discard the seeds and stem.

2. Lay the pepper pieces skin side upwards on a piece of foil under a very hot grill. Remove when the skin has blackened and wrap the pepper in the foil until cool enough to handle. Peel off the black skin and cut the pepper pieces into very thin strips.

3. Drain the butter beans and put them into a food processor or blender with 50g of butter at room temperature. Add a tablespoon of milk and whizz until smooth, gradually adding the rest of the milk. Add salt to taste.

4. Peel the garlic and slice the cloves across thinly. Put the olive oil and the remaining butter into a large pan over a fairly high heat and add the garlic and chilli. Stir for just a minute or two, or until golden brown – don't let the garlic burn. Add the butter bean mixture and simmer for 2 minutes. Remove from the heat, gradually stir in the lemon juice, and add the strips of grilled pepper.

 TIPS

○ Try this with anchovies added to the garlic, chilli and oil. It gives a fantastic extra kick and dimension to the soup.

FRIENDS & FAMILY
RECIPES

BELINDA'S CHICKEN NOODLE SOUP

A quick and healthy week-night supper (pictured on page 75).

Feeds: 4
Preparation time: 10 minutes
Cooking time: 10 minutes
♥ ✓ WF DF GF

1 litre **chicken stock**
2 free-range **chicken breasts**
2 cloves of **garlic**
200g mixed shiitake and chestnut **mushrooms**
100g **pak choi**
a large handful of **fresh coriander**
2 tablespoons **peanut oil**
200g **rice noodles**
3 tablespoons **soy sauce**
2 tablespoons **toasted sesame oil**

1. Put the chicken stock into a saucepan, put a lid on and bring to the boil. Cut the chicken breasts into small chunks.

2. Peel and finely slice the garlic. Generously slice the mushrooms. Chop the pak choi and coriander roughly.

3. Pour the peanut oil into a hot wok or wide heavy-based pan. When it smokes, add the garlic just for seconds and immediately follow with the chicken and mushrooms. Keep tossing until cooked (about 5–7 minutes). Add the soy sauce and sesame oil and keep tossing until absorbed.

4. Add the rice noodles and pak choi to the hot chicken stock, put a lid on and boil for 3–4 minutes. Pour the contents of the wok into the pan of stock and noodles and sprinkle with the coriander. Eat at once.

TIPS

- Depending on what brand of rice noodles you use, you may need to add extra stock – some soak up more juice than others.

- A squeeze of lime on top before you eat is a nice addition.

RECIPE TESTED BY SOPHIE

Belinda, my stepmother, appears effortlessly to combine managing a large extended family, a doctorate and a new career in psychology with the production of enormous feasts whenever family and friends descend upon her house (which is quite often). This is one of her staple suppers.
Henry

Belinda at Picnic Point, Summer 2009

FRIENDS & FAMILY RECIPES

BACON AND ROOT VEG SOUP

A winter warmer and a Mima staple.

Feeds: 4–6
Preparation time: 20 minutes
Cooking time: 30 minutes

✓ WF GF

100g **streaky bacon**
1 large **onion**
150g **carrots**
150g **swede**
150g **waxy potatoes**
350g **parsnips**
2 tablespoons **olive oil**
2 **bay leaves**
1.5 litres **chicken stock**
100g grated **Cheddar or Parmesan cheese**
sea salt and **freshly ground black pepper**

1. Cut the bacon into small pieces. Peel and chop the onion. Peel and dice the carrots, swede, potatoes and parsnips.

2. Heat the oil in a heavy-bottomed pan. Add the bacon and fry until it is just getting crispy. Add the onion, and cook until it is getting soft.

3. Add all the diced vegetables and the bay leaves, and cook over a gentle heat with the lid on for 10 minutes, stirring occasionally.

4. Add the stock and simmer for 15 minutes, or until the vegetables are tender.

5. Season to taste and serve in bowls, sprinkled with the cheese.

 TIPS

○ Vegetarians can use garlic instead of the bacon, and vegetable stock instead of chicken stock.

○ You can use any surplus root vegetables you have lying about. Celeriac tastes great alongside or instead of the parsnip.

RECIPE TESTED BY KATH

FROM FARMS WE TRUST

APPLE'S PERSIAN ONION SOUP

A favourite recipe from the restaurants – very healthy, and great if you are feeling under par.

Feeds: 4 as a starter
Preparation time: 10 minutes
Cooking time: 40 minutes

♥ ✓ WF DF GF

4 large **onions**
2 tablespoons **olive oil**
1 heaped teaspoon **turmeric**
1 heaped teaspoon **ground fenugreek**
1 teaspoon **dried mint**
1 litre **chicken** or **vegetable stock**
1 **cinnamon stick**
½ a **lemon**
sea salt and **freshly ground black pepper**

1. Peel the onions and slice thinly. Put the onions into a large pan with the olive oil. Add some salt and pepper, cover the pan and cook gently for at least 15 minutes, stirring occasionally.

2. Add the turmeric, fenugreek and mint, and cook for another few minutes without the lid.

3. Add the stock and cinnamon stick, bring to the boil, then reduce the heat and simmer for at least 20 minutes.

4. Add the juice of half a lemon and season with salt and pepper and serve. I like to leave the cinnamon stick in.

TIPS

○ Add some chopped fresh mint and parsley at the end to liven things up.

○ Apple adds a teaspoon of sugar for added sweetness – we leave this out.

Apple and Sophie Douglas Bate pretending to be supermodels, 2001

My best mate Sophie Douglas Bate is the most incredible chef from Edible Food Design, and we have cooked and travelled together for years. Her family used to live in Tehran and this became a staple soup in our lives – great for when you are trying to lose weight.
Apple

FRIENDS & FAMILY RECIPES

SOUP LIFTERS

Like a striking brooch on 'that old' outfit, finishing touches have the power to transform a dish. If your soup is feeling a bit flat, don't lose heart. Season it carefully and lift it with one of these toppers.

Mushroom duxelle

Crispy garlic bread-crumbs

Sliced pecans

Coriander

Rose Harissa

Crispy fried sage

Crispy parsnips

Seeds and herbs

Yoghurt

Melted onions

Grilled peppers

Spring onions

Herb butter

Golden fried garlic

Pesto

Crème fraîche

Crispy bacon

Turkish chilli flakes

Grated cheddar

Parsley

Grated Parmesan

Finely chopped courgette and carrot

Lemon zest

Toasted almonds

RICE
POTATOES
COUSCOUS
& QUINOA

THREE QUICK WAYS WITH RICE

For some reason rice seems to cause cooks an unwarranted amount of stress. Here are three super-simple ways to ease your rice-furrowed brow.

 ## FAILSAFE RICE Absorption method

Use white basmati rice.

1. Rinse the rice thoroughly in a sieve (use about 75g per person – but if you make extra you can use it to make Michelle's saffron rice cake, below).

2. Use EXACTLY 1¼ cups of water to 1 cup of rice. Put into a pan and bring to the boil.

3. Immediately turn the heat down to the lowest possible setting and cover the pan with a tight-fitting lid. It will take about 15 minutes to cook, but you can turn off the heat and leave it with the lid on for up to 40 minutes before serving.

 TIPS

o You do not need to salt the rice, but a squeeze of lemon and some butter at the end make a great seasoning.

o You can put a little oil or butter into the pan before you add the rice and gently fry a cinnamon stick with a couple of crushed cardamom pods to give an aromatic flavour. Add turmeric at this stage if you want orange rice.

 ## Michelle's CRISPY SAFFRON RICE CAKE

A simple recipe for left-over rice. Basmati works best, but you can use any kind.

1. Heat a generous knob of butter in a non-stick saucepan or frying pan, and add a good pinch of saffron (if saffron seems a bit expensive, a pinch of turmeric will do the trick).

2. Add enough rice to cover the bottom of the pan, and pack it down well. Add the rest of the rice. With a chopstick or skewer, make 3 holes to allow the steam to escape. Cover the rice with kitchen paper and a lid and put the pan on a low heat.

3. Allow to cook for 10 minutes on a low to medium heat until the base is crispy, and then turn out on to a plate.

4. The rice should be crisp on the bottom, and you should be able to turn it out on to a plate in a cake shape.

Michelle at home in London, 1979

FRIENDS & FAMILY RECIPES

③ PILAFF

There is possibly nothing more comforting than pilaff – eat it as a side dish or as a simple dinner on its own. This all-in-the-oven version is almost impossibly easy.

Feeds: 4
Preparation time: 5 minutes
Cooking time: 45 minutes
♥ ✓ WF DF GF

4 large **carrots**
2 **onions**
3 tablespoons **olive oil**
400g short-grain brown or white **rice**
800ml **chicken** or **vegetable stock**
3 **bay leaves**, fresh or dried
juice of ½ a **lemon**
a large handful of **fresh parsley**
sea salt and **freshly ground black pepper**

1. Preheat the oven to 180°C/350°F/gas mark 4. Peel the carrots and cut them into batons. Peel the onions and slice them into semicircles.

2. Put the carrots and onions into a large oven dish and add the oil, stirring to coat the vegetables. Place in the oven and cook for 20 minutes, making sure the onions don't burn.

3. Meanwhile, measure out the rice, and make your stock. Roughly chop the parsley.

4. Add the rice and bay leaves to the pan of vegetables and cover with the hot stock. The rice should be well covered, but not swimming in too much liquid.

5. Return the pan to the oven and cook for a further 25 minutes, checking regularly to make sure the rice does not cook dry. Add extra stock if it needs it.

6. When the rice is cooked and has absorbed the liquid, it should have a lovely risotto-ish texture. Add the lemon juice and chopped parsley and season well.

 TIPS

○ Pilaff is always improved by a scattering of toasted flaked almonds (or any other nuts or seeds) over the top.

○ You can use many other vegetables with this base recipe: sweet potatoes, garlic, peppers, chopped tomatoes and courgettes, for example.

○ Experiment with different herb and spice combinations with the vegetable mix.

○ Add chicken or slices of left-over lamb to make the dish more substantial.

○ Succulent sultanas always go well in a rice dish if you fancy a slightly sweet touch.

○ If you want to make it more like a risotto, you can use risotto rice. You may need to add up to 200ml extra stock for this.

RECIPE TESTED BY: LISA

RECIPE TESTED BY: DAVID

THREE QUICK WAYS WITH POTATOES

A simple boiled spud with a bit of butter and some pepper is a glorious thing – but it's worth ringing the changes. Potatoes have so much more to give.

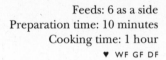

1 Baked in stock

Like a dauphinoise, but without the cream. You can experiment with herb, spice and vegetable combinations. The recipe below is one of our favourites.

POTATOES LEON-AISE

Feeds: 6 as a side
Preparation time: 10 minutes
Cooking time: 1 hour
♥ WF GF DF

1.3kg **potatoes**
2 large **onions**
1 bulb of **garlic**
½ a **lemon**
5 **fresh bay leaves**
80ml **extra virgin olive oil**
650ml **chicken stock**
sea salt and **freshly ground black pepper**

1. Preheat the oven to 180°C/350°F/gas mark 4.

2. Wash the potatoes thoroughly, and slice thinly with their skins still on.

3. Peel and slice the onions finely. Slice the garlic bulb thinly crossways (leaving the skin on). Slice the lemon half as finely as you can muster.

4. Toss everything except the stock into a baking tray. Season well. Pat down so it fits snugly. Pour in the stock – it should come about halfway up the potatoes.

5. Place them in the oven for 1 hour, or until cooked.

2 Boiled, then dressed

Boil your spuds as usual, but instead of a simple coating of butter and pepper, finish them with panache. The Warm Anchovy, Garlic & Potato Salad (page 158) is one example. Our two other favourites are:

Crispy Garlic and Ginger Let the potatoes steam dry in the colander, then fry them in a pan with chopped garlic and ginger until all the ingredients go golden and crispy. (This is a great way to treat left-over cooked potatoes from the fridge.)

Tangy Parsley Sauce Melt some butter in a pan. Add finely chopped parsley and a dash of vinegar. Season and pour over the spuds.

3 Chopped small and roasted

There are lots of fast, delicious variations on Pierre's Potatoes (see page 135). The essential moves are: chop your raw potatoes small, put plenty of oil in a roasting tin, get it spitting hot in the oven before you add the potatoes, then put the tray back in and cook them fast and hot. These are some of our favourite embellishments:

Traditional Woody herbs and whole cloves of garlic.

Meaty Little chunks of chorizo or pieces of sausage.

Bay More fresh bay leaves than you would ever imagine (e.g. about 15 in baking tray).

Spanish Sweet paprika and sliced onions.

THREE QUICK WAYS WITH SWEET POTATOES

We have had a love affair with this sweet, soft tuber since we first opened our doors.

ROAST SWEET POTATOES

1. Preheat the oven to 180–200°C/350–400°F/gas mark 4–6.

2. Cut your sweet potatoes into thick wedges with the skin on. Place them in a large baking tray.

3. Scatter over a tablespoon of ground cumin or ground coriander, or chilli flakes (or all three).

4. Season with salt and pepper and toss in a generous dash of olive oil.

5. Put into the oven for 30 minutes, or until cooked and slightly crispy.

ANDI'S SWEET POTATO FRIES

Finally a healthy(ish) chip.

1. Finely slice your sweet potatoes into elegant slim chips, leaving the skins on.

2. Fry small batches in hot vegetable oil until golden.

3. Drain, scatter with sea salt and eat immediately.

BAKED SWEET POTATOES
with numerous stuffings

1. Heat the oven to around 180°C/350°F/gas mark 4. Bake whole for around 1 hour, or until soft.

2. Split the potatoes open and stuff.

Stuffings we like include:

- Home-made hummus
- Tsatsiki
- Feta cheese and spring onions
- Crème fraîche and za'tar
- Yoghurt and harissa

Andi, Cyprus 1972

FRIENDS & FA
RECIPES

Andi lives around the corner from me in Hackney. She has a smile that could power the national grid and, man, can she cook. I had been trying and failing to get sweet potato chips to be crispy for months when she came round with this recipe to relieve my pain. The trick is to cut them very fine, cook them in hot, hot oil, and eat them immediately. *Henry*

Sweet potatoes are one of those vegetables (along with carrots) where buying organic makes a real difference to flavour. The tubers are smaller, more dense and have a deep intensity of flavour.

Clockwise from the top: Roast Sweet Potatoes; Andi's Sweet Potato Fries; Baked Sweet Potatoes

THREE QUICK WAYS WITH COUSCOUS, BULGAR & QUINOA

Although the first two of these are forms of wheat and the latter is an unprocessed grain unto itself, you can use these three beauties interchangeably. Feel free to switch the grains in the recipes below. (If you don't fancy wheat, most big supermarkets now stock the traditional Moroccan barley couscous too.)

Grain salads

1. Cook the grain as per the instructions on the packet. (For couscous and bulgar, you can usually just pour over boiling stock or water and leave to soak, but quinoa will take a bit more cooking.)

2. Mix in olive oil, lemon juice, seasoning and your choice of additional ingredients. We like pine nuts, dried apricots, rocket leaves, finely sliced red onion and fresh parsley; or olives, flash-fried courgettes and aubergines, 'Sun-dried' Tomatoes (see page 267) and fresh mint.

However, we have a particular soft spot for this recipe – and for its creator, our friend Laura.

LAURA'S JEWELLED SALAD

Feeds: 4
Preparation time: 5 minutes
Cooking time: 5 minutes
♥ WF V

200g **barley couscous**
200g good-quality **feta cheese**
1 **cucumber**
a bunch of **mixed fresh green herbs**,
    e.g. **mint** and **coriander**
100g **pine nuts**
seeds of 1 large **pomegranate**
2 cloves of **garlic**
2 tablespoons **extra virgin olive oil**
juice of 1½ **lemons**
sea salt and **freshly ground black pepper**

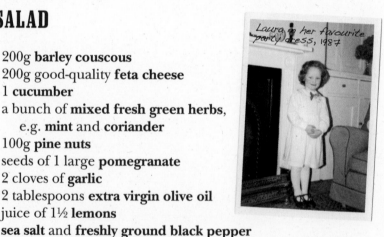

Laura in her favourite party dress, 1987

1. Prepare the couscous as per the instructions on the packet. Leave to cool in a large bowl.

2. Crumble the feta and cut the cucumber into chunks. Add these to the bowl, then roughly tear the herbs and add them too.

3. Lightly toast the pine nuts in a frying pan over a low heat, and scatter these and the pomegranate seeds over the salad.

4. Peel and finely mince or grate the garlic. Whisk together the olive oil, lemon juice and garlic and pour over the salad. Season well with salt and pepper, and serve.

FRIENDS & FAMILY RECIPES

② Grain pilaffs

For something a little more substantial, you can also treat your grains as you would rice in a pilaff. Simply roast any left-over vegetables you have, then cook them with the grains in stock. This recipe came to us via Henry's wife, Mima, whose sister Hattie picked it up from her friend Lucy, whose mother used to live in Cyprus. A typically picaresque recipe journey.

HATTIE'S POURGOURI

Feeds: 4
Preparation time: 5 minutes
Cooking time: 20 minutes
♥ DF V

2 small **onions** (or 1 large)
3 cloves of **garlic**
a handful of **fresh mint**, **flat-leaf parsley** or **coriander**
3 tablespoons **olive oil**
250g **bulgar wheat**
2 x 400g tins of **chopped tomatoes**
a handful of **almonds**, **pistachios** or **pine nuts**
sea salt and **freshly ground black pepper**

1. Peel the onions and garlic and chop finely. Chop the herbs.

2. Heat the oil in a thick-bottomed pan. Add the onions and garlic and cook for 5 minutes.

3. Add the bulgar wheat, stir well and add the chopped tomatoes. Stir thoroughly and lower the heat. Put a lid on the pan and cook gently for 15 minutes, stirring regularly, as it can stick easily.

4. When the bulgar is soft, add salt, pepper and the chopped herbs.

5. Toast the nuts in a frying pan and scatter them over the top when you are ready to eat.

 TIPS

○ Drizzle over extra olive oil if necessary.

○ Delicious with Greek yoghurt, and brilliant served with roast lamb.

○ As good cold as it is hot.

③ Grains in soups

Adding grains towards the end of cooking is a great way to bulk up your soups. You will need to add them at slightly different times before you serve them. As a guide:

○ Couscous   less than 3 minutes

○ Bulgar   10 minutes

○ Quinoa   15 minutes

Hattie's Pourgouri (above); Laura's Jewelled Salad (below)

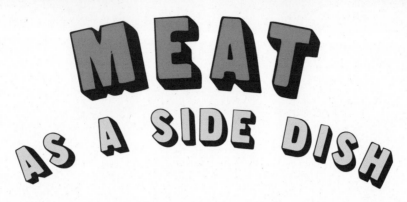

MEAT AS A SIDE DISH

As we mentioned at the start of the vegetable section, it pays to think of the meat dish as a side to the vegetables rather than vice versa. Not in a bad way, you understand. Think of Elizabeth Taylor snuggled into the sidecar of a classic Triumph.

If you are concentrating your energies on the vegetables, you want to spend less time and money on the meat. Here are some ways that we go about that.

1 **Smash, dash and flash** – A quick way to tackle a small amount of a cheaper cut of any meat. Slice into 1cm thick slices then wrap in clingfilm and give it a good whack with a rolling pin until it is at least half the thickness. The thinner the better as this is just meant to be a flash of taste, and thinly cut pieces of chicken for example can carry more flavour than a big chunk. Cut the pieces into credit-card-sized pieces, and dip (or dash) them into a strong flavouring – e.g. a shop-bought garam masala, curry powder or Indian paste. Season with sea salt and freshly ground black pepper. Flash fry or grill at a high heat for a minute or so on each side. Squeeze on some lemon before serving.

2 **Left-overs** – Buy a slightly bigger roast than you need for the weekend and you'll have meat side dishes for the next week. Chicken can be reheated in a little stock, with some frozen peas thrown in and Parmesan grated on top (see picture opposite). Left-over lamb makes a soothing pilaf (see page 87). And just about any left-over meat can be chopped finely and fried up with garlic and ginger paste and green herbs.

3 **A slice of sausage** – Buy a really good fresh chorizo and grill a little for the side. This also goes for standard sausages, which, sliced into 2cm rounds and fried till crisp with fennel seeds, make a great meat garnish (see picture opposite).

4 **Marvellous meals with mince** – Fry a little mince with some ground cumin, salt and pepper in a pan until nicely brown with some crispy bits. (If you like, add pine nuts, onions and garlic). Sprinkle it over a tinned bean salad, some green beans, or a shop-bought hummus. (You can use this same topper approach with little bits of bacon – great on broad beans – see picture – or broken up sausage.)

5 **Offaly good** – If you are an offal lover, a whole other world of cheap and tasty meat is open to you. You can't beat the classics: 'devilled' kidneys fried with Worcestershire sauce, butter, cayenne and mustard (see picture opposite); or fried chicken livers with sherry vinegar and parsley.

6 **The white stuff** – It is still possible to buy cheap, fresh, sustainable white fish. Think coley, whiting and pollock. But these need something to add flavour. Buy fillets and treat them as the meat above but without the bashing.

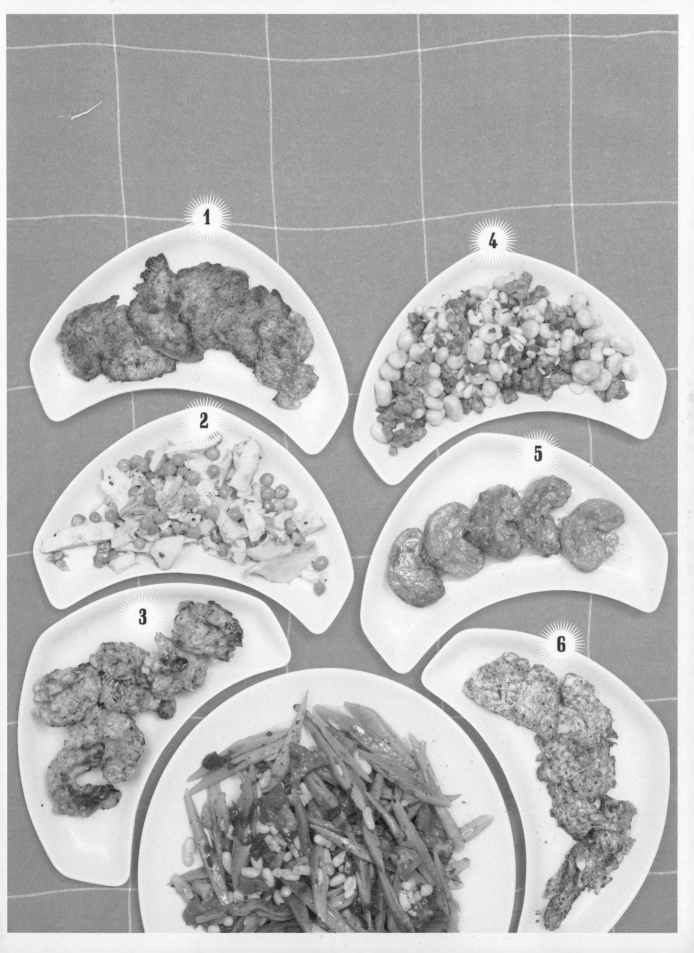

There is a reason why curries have become the nation's favourite meals, and it's not just because they go brilliantly with beer. The bold spices of Eastern cuisine can work miracles on just about any base ingredient, from chicken and fish to pulses. Go easy on the ghee, moreover, and you'll find they make you healthy and beautiful, too.

COCONUT CHICKEN & *petit pois curry*

A fantastically quick curry to make.

Feeds: 4–6
Preparation time: 10 minutes
Cooking time: 15 minutes
✓ WF GF

6 **chicken breasts**
25g **butter**
2 teaspoons **nigella seeds** (black onion seeds)
2 tablespoons **tikka paste**
300ml **coconut milk**
200g **frozen peas**
a handful of **fresh coriander leaves**
sea salt and **freshly ground black pepper**

1. Slice the chicken breasts into thin strips.

2. Melt the butter in a heavy frying pan. Add the chicken and nigella seeds and cook for between 8–10 minutes, or until the chicken is cooked through.

3. Stir in the tikka paste, coconut milk and peas. Bring gently to the boil, stirring all the time, and simmer for a minute or two.

4. Chop the coriander, add to the pan and season to taste.

TIPS

○ All the ingredients for this lightning recipe can be kept in your freezer or storecupboard, so grab the chicken on your way home and you can be eating a delicious creamy curry within minutes.

○ Basmati rice, which takes 10 minutes to cook, completes the meal.

Clockwise from the top: Dalston Sweet Potato Curry: Coconut Chicken with Petit Pois; Jossy's Chicken Liver Curry

FRIENDS & FAMILY RECIPES

After a visit to Vietnam decades ago, I longed for the comforting richness of coconut milk in my home cooking. However, at that time the only possibility was to laboriously make your own from fresh or desiccated coconut; these days tins are available here for instant transformation to spicy dishes. Peas are found in so many Indian dishes that it is surprising no other cuisine seems to have realized how well they go with spices, and in my view the only way to enjoy chicken breasts is thinly sliced and strongly flavoured. *Jossy*

97

JOSSY'S CHICKEN LIVER CURRY

One for the liver lovers – tangy and meaty and very cheap (pictured on page 96).

Feeds: 4–6
Preparation time: 20 minutes
Cooking time: 35 minutes
✓ WF GF

800g **chicken livers**
3 tablespoons **natural yoghurt**
2 medium **onions**
3 cloves of **garlic**
2.5cm piece of **fresh ginger**
2 tablespoons **tikka paste**
3 tablespoons **lemon juice**
25g **butter**
1 teaspoon **cumin seeds**
1 x 400g tin of **chopped tomatoes**
a large handful of **fresh coriander leaves**
sea salt and **freshly ground black pepper**

1. Cut the chicken livers into 2.5cm pieces (removing any sinewy bits), place in a bowl, add the yoghurt and set aside.

2. Peel the onions, garlic and ginger and roughly chop. Put one of the onions into a blender with the garlic, ginger, tikka paste and lemon juice and whizz to a paste.

3. Tip the mixture into a casserole dish, place over a low heat and simmer gently for about 15 minutes, stirring frequently.

4. Finely slice the remaining onion and add to the pan with the butter, cumin seeds, chicken livers and tomatoes. Simmer for a further 15 minutes, stirring occasionally.

5. Season with roughly chopped coriander and salt and pepper to taste.

 TIPS

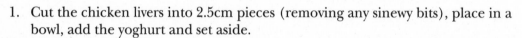

o Best served with basmati rice and a salad.

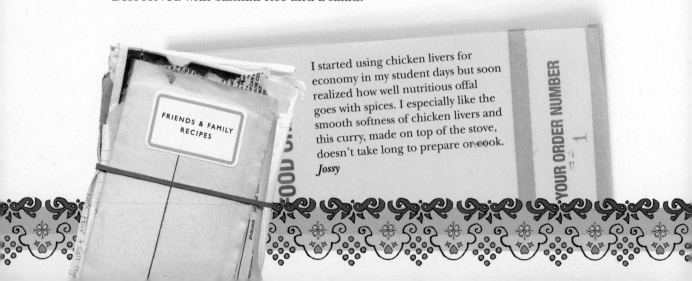

I started using chicken livers for economy in my student days but soon realized how well nutritious offal goes with spices. I especially like the smooth softness of chicken livers and this curry, made on top of the stove, doesn't take long to prepare or cook.
Jossy

FRIENDS & FAMILY RECIPES

YOUR ORDER NUMBER

DALSTON SWEET POTATO CURRY

A sweet, rich, everyday vegetable curry (pictured on page 96).

Feeds: 6
Preparation time: 15 minutes
Cooking time: 40 minutes
✓ WF DF GF V

1 **onion**
1 tablespoon **sunflower oil**
4 cloves of **garlic**
2.5cm piece of **fresh ginger**
2 teaspoons **ground coriander**
2 teaspoons **ground cumin**
½–1 teaspoon **cayenne pepper**, depending how hot you like it
1 level teaspoon **turmeric**
1 x 400g tin of **chopped tomatoes**
4 **sweet potatoes** (not the giant ones)
1 **cauliflower**
1 x 400g tin of **coconut milk**
100g **cashew nuts**
sea salt and **freshly ground black pepper**

1. Peel the onion, roughly chop and fry gently in the oil in a large saucepan for 5 minutes. Peel and grate the garlic and ginger, add to the pan and fry for 1 minute. Add the spices and cook for a further 2 minutes, until they are fragrant.

2. Add the tomatoes, and the peeled and cubed sweet potatoes. Cook for about 30 minutes, adding water if it seems to be drying out.

3. Divide the cauliflower into florets and add them to the pan with the coconut milk. Put the lid on and simmer for around 8 minutes, or until soft.

4. Meanwhile, gently toast the cashew nuts in a dry frying pan.

5. Season to taste and add the nuts just before serving

TIPS

○ Add spinach, coriander or peas for a bit of colour.

○ Serve with rice and a blob of yoghurt.

Mima has a tiny drop of Indian blood in her, which means she feels entitled to invent curries willy-nilly. This one has become a staple supper at home in Dalston. *Henry*

Mima in Egypt, 2005

FRIENDS & FAMILY RECIPES

KERALAN FISH CURRY

This is a simple south Indian fish curry.

Feeds: 4
Preparation time: 10 minutes
Cooking time: 20 minutes
✓ WF DF GF

1 **fresh green chilli**
1 teaspoon **rapeseed oil**, to make the paste
1 teaspoon **ground coriander**
½ teaspoon **turmeric**
5 cloves of **garlic**
2.5cm piece of **fresh ginger**
1 tablespoon **coconut oil** or **rapeseed oil**
½ teaspoon **fenugreek seeds**
4 small **onions**
100ml **coconut milk**
400g **mackerel fillets**, cut into 5cm pieces
sea salt and freshly ground **black pepper**

1. Deseed the chilli and put it into a blender with the rapeseed oil, coriander, turmeric, and peeled garlic and ginger and whizz to form a paste.

2. Heat the coconut oil in a pan and sauté the paste and the fenugreek seeds.

3. Peel the onions, slice finely and add them to the pan with the coconut milk and 300ml of water. Season really well with salt and pepper. Bring to the boil and keep it at a gentle boil until the sauce reduces, which should take about 5 minutes.

4. Cut the mackerel into 5cm pieces and add to the curry. Simmer gently until the fish is cooked through, which should take between 5 and 8 minutes.

TIPS

o Best served with rice.

o You can use prawns or white fish if mackerel is too strong for your taste.

o The mackerel should be very fresh, as it develops too strong a flavour if kept for too long in the fridge.

Honeymoon Vegetable Curry (above); Keralan Fish Curry (below)

HONEYMOON VEGETABLE CURRY

Not the most beautiful of curries, but a great staple for a simple healthy supper (pictured on page 100).

Feeds: 4
Preparation time: 15 minutes
Cooking time: 20 minutes
✓ WF DF GF V

4 **courgettes**
2 **carrots**
2 **aubergines**
¼ of an **onion**
2 **fresh green chillies**
200ml **coconut milk**
½ teaspoon **ground cumin**
¼ teaspoon **turmeric**
1 **lime**
sea salt and **freshly ground black pepper**

RECIPE TESTED BY MATILDA

1. Chop the courgettes into diagonal slices. Peel and chop the carrots into chunky batons and chop the aubergines into cubes. Peel and chop the onion roughly, and deseed the chillies.

2. Place the coconut milk, chillies, onion and cumin into a food processor and whizz to a paste.

3. Dry fry the turmeric in a pan for a minute, then add the vegetables and 200ml of water. Bring to the boil, then reduce the heat and simmer for about 15 minutes, or until tender.

4. Add the coconut milk paste and cook gently for another 5 minutes.

5. Season, and squeeze over the juice of the lime before serving.

TIPS

o Serve on white basmati rice.

Mima and I went to Kerala, in southern India, for our honeymoon, largely because we knew the food would be really tasty. We were not disappointed. At the Coconut Lagoon, a swanky eco-hotel on a lake, the in-house entertainment included a tour of the hotel's composting system or lunchtime cookery lessons with the resident chef. We did both, and brought this recipe home as a souvenir (of the food, not the composter). *Henry*

Mima and Henry on their Keralan honeymoon, 2006

SOUTH INDIAN PEPPER CHICKEN

The trick with this dish is to be bold with the pepper – remember it is an ingredient, not a seasoning (pictured on page 104).

Feeds: 2
Preparation time: 15 minutes
Cooking time: 20–25 minutes
♥ ✓ WF DF GF

500g **chicken thighs**
1 tablespoon **olive oil**
4 cloves of **garlic**
2.5cm piece of **fresh ginger**
1 **onion**
2 **tomatoes**
1 teaspoon **turmeric**
a small handful of **fresh coriander leaves**
sea salt and lots of **freshly ground black pepper**

About five years ago we travelled with our friend Gowri to Kerala and Tamil Nadu, where we were looked after by her family. Most of the best dishes in the south of India are vegetarian (worthy of a whole Leon book, maybe), but this was a chicken dish that satisfied our carnivorous cravings. Henry has recreated it for this book.
John and Katie

1. Cut each chicken thigh into 2 or 3 pieces with a heavy knife. Season with a lot of pepper and some salt, then add some more pepper.

2. Heat the oil in a pan and brown the chicken, turning it a few times to ensure a good colour. Remove the chicken from the pan.

3. Peel and finely chop the garlic and ginger. Slice the onions. Cut the tomatoes into rough 1cm dice.

4. Add the ginger, garlic, onions and turmeric to the pan and fry for a couple of minutes. Add the tomatoes and a couple of tablespoons of water. Cover, turn down the heat and simmer for 2 minutes.

5. Put the chicken back into the pan, cover with a lid and cook till tender. Season, and stir in the chopped coriander leaves.

TIPS

o Goes very well with some rice and a good TV programme.

Kate and Gowri in Kerala, 2005

Cruising on a houseboat, Kerala, 2005

SPICE FRIED FISH *with red onion*

This is a quick fish dish that works well as a side with a spread of vegetable dishes.

Feeds: 4
Preparation time: 5 minutes
Cooking time: 15 minutes
♥ ✓ DF

2 teaspoons **coriander seed**
2 teaspoons **cumin seed**
2 teaspoons **black peppercorns**
2 teaspoons **black mustard seed**
2 tablespoons **buckwheat** or **plain flour**
a handful of crushed **cashews**
2 **red onions**
6 tablespoons **rapeseed oil**
400g **sustainable white fish**
sea salt and **freshly ground black pepper**

1. Mix the coriander, cumin, peppercorns and mustard seed with 2 teaspoons of sea salt and grind to a powder (best done in a clean coffee grinder). Put into a bowl and add the buckwheat flour. Check the seasoning. The flavour should be strong.

2. Put your widest frying pan on to a high heat and toast the crushed cashews. Remove them from the pan and set aside.

3. Peel the onions and slice as finely as you can. Add them to the pan with 2 tablespoons of the oil. Cook over a high heat, stirring continually so that they get a good colour and start to soften. Season, and remove the onions from the pan.

4. Add the rest of the oil to the pan. Cut the fish fillets into rough credit-card-sized pieces, toss in the flour mix and shallow fry them until crisp and brown (about 2 minutes on each side). Unless you have a monster pan you will need to do this in batches.

5. Put the fish on a serving plate and sprinkle over the onions and nuts.

TIPS

o Use any cheap sustainable white fish – coley, whiting, pollock and pouting all work well.

o If you don't have the individual spices, substitute 3 teaspoons of garam masala.

o Experiment with your own spice combinations. Add some chilli to the spice mix if you like it fiery.

o This works well with a little chopped fresh coriander sprinkled on top.

o If you don't want to fry the onions, try just thinly slicing them and dressing them with lime juice and a touch of salt.

South Indian Pepper Chicken (above); Spice Fried Fish with Red Onion (below)

JOHN'S THAI CURRY

The green chicken curry has become the chicken tikka masala of the western Thai restaurant scene. You can replicate it in your own home very easily and quickly, thanks to the Thai curry pastes available. However, be sure to steer well clear of ready-made sauces: they will leave you disappointed. Use only a high quality paste and start from there.

Feeds: 4
Preparation time: 15 minutes
Cooking time: 15 minutes
✓ WF DF GF

4 **chicken thighs**
1 tablespoon **olive oil**
2–3 tablespoons **Thai curry paste**
1 x 400ml tin of **coconut milk**
1 x 225g tin of **bamboo shoots**
100g **Thai aubergines**
2 tablespoons **Thai fish sauce**
a few leaves of **fresh Thai sweet basil**
sea salt and **freshly ground black pepper**

1. Remove the meat from the chicken thighs and cut into thin strips.

2. Heat the olive oil in a large frying pan, add the Thai curry paste, and stir the paste into the oil as you fry on a hot heat for a minute.

3. Gradually add the coconut milk, followed by the chicken.

4. Drain and add the bamboo shoots, the Thai aubergines and simmer for 10 minutes.

5. Add the fish sauce, then taste and adjust the seasoning with salt and pepper if you want to.

6. Sprinkle the curry with fresh sweet basil and serve.

 TIPS

I first tasted Green Chicken Curry not in Thailand but at college when a small Thai restaurant opened in the town. I thought it was one of the tastiest things I had ever eaten. Nowadays, it's a dish that most of us have tasted and it is a staple dish on most British 'food service' restaurants and pubs. But many restaurants who are not authentically Thai seem to get it wrong and the sauces you can buy in supermarkets are no better. Having had the chance to visit Thailand a couple of times, I can confirm the view of many others that there are few better things than sitting on a Thai beach eating this dish, maybe with a Phad Thai too. *John*

o If you cannot find Thai sweet basil, use normal basil instead.

o Serve with sticky rice, jasmine rice or even brown rice.

o Get the right paste (I recommend Mae Ploy), and don't buy the sauces that come in jars.

o The chicken will cook more quickly and taste much better if it is cut into thin strips rather than big chunks.

o Add the coconut milk slowly, and stir as you do so to avoid the paste and the coconut milk separating.

o Thai aubergines are nothing like the aubergines we are used to. You can buy them in larger supermarkets or Thai shops in jars. If you cannot find them, you can add peas instead.

Corner Shop Classics

In most urban neighbourhoods, the fourth emergency service is the corner shop. Nestling between *Heat* magazine and lottery tickets, you can generally find enough staple ingredients to rustle together a tasty meal – even at the most modest store.

Here are some of our favourite 999 meals for when the cupboard is completely bare.

ULTIMATE CHEESE ON TOAST ✓✓ ᵛ

When done well, nothing can beat the bubbling crispy brown homeliness of this dish. Keep a good, seedy sliced bread in your freezer and toast it slice by slice.

This recipe is very hard to beat.

1. A good bread, toasted.

2. Butter, spread on the toast.

3. Dijon mustard, spread on top of the butter.

4. Fine slices of tomato, in one layer on top of the mustard.

5. Cheddar cheese (a good one if you have it), sliced into pieces the thickness of a hardback book cover and laid on top of the tomato, 2 slices deep.

6. A good fresh grind of black pepper.

7. Put under the grill until melted and starting to bubble and brown.

8. Splash on some Worcestershire sauce.

9. Eat on its own or with baked beans.

Variations on a theme

○ **Cheese and Onion:** Grate the cheese and mix it with some finely sliced onion.

○ **Hot Horseradish:** Replace the Dijon mustard with some horseradish sauce.

○ **Cheese on Sea:** Slice a tinned sardine in half and put it on top of the tomatoes before adding the cheese.

Hawk (left) and Tuzuk (a.k.a. Şahin and Suleyman) at Greenwood Road Costcutter, Henry's local corner shop

ULTIMATE MUSHROOMS ON TOAST ✓ᵥ

A chef friend of ours once said that he believed the common button mushroom would be an expensive delicacy if it was rare. The way that it colours and deepens in flavour as it cooks is a wonder. Don't feel you need fancy mushrooms to make the ultimate mushrooms on toast.

1. A good bread, toasted.

2. Butter, spread on the toast.

3. A good knob of butter and a trickle of vegetable oil in a hot pan. The butter should foam.

4. A generous handful of sliced button mushrooms thrown into the pan with a tablespoon of finely sliced onion. Don't move them around too much. Toss every 30 seconds or so, but give them time to go golden. Season.

5. Finely chopped garlic and fresh parsley thrown in for the last 30 seconds.

6. A squeeze of lemon juice and on to the toast.

Variations on a theme

○ **Luxury:** Instead of lemon juice add a splash of white wine at the end. When this has bubbled off, add a tablespoon of double cream and bubble for 20 seconds before offloading on to the toast.

○ **Meaty:** Before you cook the mushrooms, fry some prosciutto in the pan until it goes crispy. Stick it on top like a shark's fin.

○ **Toast on Mushrooms on Toast:** This was an accident we discovered while photographing the pictures for this book. Nothing in the world tastes better. Fry some breadcrumbs with garlic and seasoning until they are crispy. Make the Ultimate Mushrooms on Toast. Sprinkle the garlic breadcrumbs on top for extra crunch.

BEAN SALAD *with quick pickled onions*

Simple, fresh and healthy – pickling the onions like this sweetens them and takes away the raw onion flavour.

Feeds: 4
Preparation time: 15 minutes
Cooking time: 0 minutes
♥ ✓ WF DF GF V

1 clove of **garlic**
1 **lemon**
a large handful of chopped **fresh flat-leaf parsley**
1 large **red onion**
2 medium **vine-ripened tomatoes**
2 tablespoons **extra virgin olive oil**
2 x 400g tins of **cannellini beans**
sea salt and **freshly ground black pepper**

1. Peel the garlic. On the finest holes of your grater, grate the garlic and lemon zest and mix it in a small bowl with the chopped parsley.

2. Peel the red onion and slice as finely as you can. Put the slices into a bowl with a few pinches of sea salt and the lemon juice. Leave for 5 minutes.

3. Chop the tomatoes into rough chunks. Season with salt and add them to the onions, along with the olive oil and the drained beans. Toss really well to combine the flavours. Season.

4. Leave the salad to sit until you get a nice pooling of tomato juice at the bottom – the magic juice. This will take around 5–10 minutes.

5. When ready to eat, stir in the parsley, lemon and garlic mix, and serve.

 TIPS

o Serve with sourdough toast for a simple supper.

o Add toasted seeds or almonds.

o Substitute other fresh green herbs for the parsley.

o There are three things that raise this dish above the ordinary: the pickled onions; letting it sit so the juices steep; and the raw parsley, lemon and garlic mix at the end. You can try all sorts of combinations of different beans and vegetables (raw, grated courgettes are a great addition, as is grated carrot).

Bean Salad with Quick Pickled Onions (above); Quick Bean & Lettuce Stew (below)

QUICK BEAN & LETTUCE STEW

For days when you have no time, but want something that's properly nourishing (pictured on page 112).

Feeds: 4
Preparation time: 5 minutes
Cooking time: 15 minutes
♥ ✓ WF DF GF

6 rashers of **bacon**
2 cloves of **garlic**
4 tablespoons **olive oil**
¼ teaspoon **fennel seeds**
1 x 400g tin of **chopped tomatoes**
200ml **chicken stock**
1 x 400g tin of **cannellini beans** (235g when drained)
150g cos **lettuce**
sea salt and **freshly ground black pepper**

1. Chop the bacon and garlic. Heat the olive oil in a pan and add the bacon. Cook for a few minutes, then add the chopped garlic and fennel seeds.

2. Pour in the tinned tomatoes and cook on a high heat for 5 minutes.

3. Add the stock and the drained beans, and cook for a further 5 minutes.

4. Season well, add the chopped lettuce, and allow it to wilt before serving.

5. Drizzle with olive oil and sprinkle with lots of black pepper.

 TIPS

o This works with all sorts of beans.

o If you want to make it a vegetarian dish, replace the bacon with a few chopped black olives.

RECIPE TESTED BY · LISA & HARRY

RECIPE TESTED BY · DAVINA

HATTIE'S SWEET ONION FRITTATA

This is a very economical and cheap meal to have with salad and a chunk of bread (pictured on page 116).

Feeds: 4
Preparation time: 15 minutes
Cooking time: 30 minutes
✓ WF GF V

800g **onions**
a handful of **fresh flat-leaf parsley**
50g **butter**
8 large **eggs**
sea salt and **freshly ground black pepper**

1. Peel the onions and slice into thin semicircles. Roughly chop the parsley. Melt the butter in a large frying pan and add the onions. Cook over a gentle heat, covered with a lid if you have one, for 25 minutes, or until the onions are soft and sweet. Meanwhile, preheat the grill to a medium heat.

2. Crack the eggs into a bowl and mix well, adding salt and pepper to taste.

3. Add the onion mixture to the eggs, mix well and add the chopped parsley. Return the mixture to the pan that the onions were cooking in, or a smaller one if the original is wide and will make the frittata too shallow.

4. Very gently cook the frittata on the hob, watching carefully so as not to let it burn on the bottom. When you think it's cooked through, apart from the top, which will still be runny, place it under the grill to finish off the top.

5. Allow to cool to lukewarm, and serve with a green salad.

 TIPS

○ Grated Parmesan is a good addition to the egg mixture. You can mix any left-over vegetables with the onions, too. Peas and peppers go well, as do cold potatoes and any old ends of cheese that you might want to use up.

○ To make this into a quiche or tart, line a 25cm flan tin with puff or short crust pastry (if using short crust pastry you will need to bake it blind for 15 minutes in the preheated oven first). Add the onion filling and bake it in the oven at 180°C/350°F/gas mark 4 for 25–30 minutes or until golden and firm.

Hattie picnicking, 1979

PRIORITY
This easy and economical dish has been a staple in our household for years. It is very easy and every time we make it we find ourselves adding new bits to it. We even made vast amounts for our wedding party and they went down a treat.
Hattie

RECIPE TESTED BY JACKIE & AMY

FRIENDS & FAMILY RECIPES

JOHN DERHAM'S STUFFED PEPPERS

Allow one whole tomato per half of red pepper.

Feeds: 4 (as a side)
Preparation time: 10 minutes
Cooking time: 30 minutes

♥ ✓ WF DF GF

RECIPE TESTED BY JANE

2 large **red peppers**
4 **tomatoes**
4 cloves of **garlic**
2 tablespoons **extra virgin olive oil**
8 **anchovy fillets**
sea salt and **freshly ground black pepper**

John Derham (Katie's Dad) and John's brother Tom, 1958

1. Preheat the oven to 240°C/475°F/gas mark 8.

2. Halve and deseed the peppers.

3. Remove the cores from the tomatoes and pour over boiling water, leave for 2 minutes, then drain and plunge into cold water. When cool, peel off the skins, and put 1 tomato into each pepper half.

4. Crush the garlic and spread under and over the tomatoes as they sit in the peppers. Drizzle with olive oil and season with salt and pepper.

5. Lay 2 anchovy fillets over each tomato, and bake in the oven for 30 minutes, turning the oven temperature down to 200°C/400°F/ gas mark 6 after the first 10 minutes.

This classic French recipe was first brought to this country by Elizabeth David in her book *Italian Food*. So simple, yet so good. This is Katie's dad John's take on it. Ripe in-season peppers are essential. When Katie and I were first going out we would spend weekends at her mum and dad's house in Wilmslow and John would, with a glass of wine always somewhere close by, make great dinners for the family. This dish is one John often includes in his repertoire, making it while listening to Cuban music in high fidelity.
John

JOHN'S FRIED AUBERGINES

RECIPE TESTED BY LISA

Feeds: 4
Preparation time: 5 minutes
Cooking time: 20 minutes

♥ ✓ WF DF GF V

700g **aubergines**
3 cloves of **garlic**
4 tablespoons **extra virgin olive oil**
8 tablespoons **light olive oil** or **vegetable oil**
juice of ½ a **lemon**
sea salt and **freshly ground black pepper**

1. Cut the tops off the aubergines and slice each one lengthways into 5mm thick slices. Place on a baking tray and sprinkle liberally with salt.

2. Leave for 5 minutes to draw the moisture out, then rinse the slices under the tap and dry thoroughly with kitchen paper.

3. Peel and finely mince or grate the garlic and put into a clean bowl with the extra virgin olive oil and some pepper.

4. Get your largest frying pan on a medium heat, and fry the aubergine in batches in the light olive oil, until golden brown and soft, turning them over half way through.

5. When the aubergines are cooked, place them on a plate and dress with the garlic oil and a squeeze of lemon juice.

Katie and I made this dish many times just after we got married in 1999, so we tend to associate it with TV dinners in our small flat in Paddington, probably watching *Sex and the City* or some other late-Nineties US show. We used to eat it with the Stuffed Peppers and together these form the basis of a great flavourful vegetable-based dinner. Left-overs of both can be popped into a lunchbox for the next day.
John

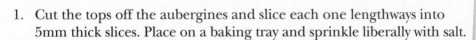

Clockwise from left: John's Fried Aubergines; Hattie's Sweet Onion Frittata; John Derham's Stuffed Peppers

TOM'S RED PESTO SURPRISE

Ideal comfort food, and perfect for curing a lingering hangover. No one has quite worked out what the surprise is yet.

Feeds: 4
Preparation time: 5 minutes
Cooking time: 20 minutes
DF

5 cloves of **garlic**
2 **onions**
250g **smoked streaky bacon**
3 tablespoons **olive oil**
350g **frozen peas**
400g **penne**
3–4 tablespoons good **red pesto**

1. Put a pan of salted water on to boil. Peel and finely chop the garlic and onions, and cut the bacon into small chunks.

2. Fry the garlic and onions in the olive oil in a large heavy-based frying pan for 5 minutes. Add the chopped bacon and cook for a further 3 minutes. Add the peas and stir well, coating them well with oil, then cook for around 10 minutes on a slow heat.

3. While the sauce is simmering, cook your pasta according to the instructions on the packet, and drain, retaining 1 tablespoon of the cooking water. Put the pasta back into the pan with the reserved water to keep it moist.

4. When the peas are cooked and you are ready to eat, stir in the pesto. Add the pasta, and stir well. Serve immediately.

TIPS

o The key is not to be mean with your pesto. If you feel it needs more, add more.

Tom and Ned in Hackney, December 2009

I discovered this dish while working in a City law firm and living in Clerkenwell with another burnt-out lawyer friend (who has also left the City well behind and now runs a rather fine pub). For a while we ate little else, as it was so easy (neither of us having any culinary skills whatsoever) and so completely addictive. I still can't get enough of it, although I probably overdo it on the bacon and red pesto. *Tom*

IMMEDIATE

FRIENDS & FAMILY RECIPES

THE FRIDGE IS BARE.

YOU FORGOT TO STOP OFF AT THE CORNER SHOP ON YOUR WAY HOME.

YOU DON'T HAVE THE CASH FOR A DELIVERY.

THESE ARE THE RECIPES THAT WILL HELP YOU LIVE TO FIGHT ANOTHER DAY.

THESE ARE OUR STORE CUPBOARD STAPLES.

PASTA WITH PEAS

Even in the depths of a nuclear winter, you could probably rustle together the ingredients for this dish – unsophisticated but cosy, perfect for a TV dinner.

Feeds: 4
Preparation time: 5 minutes
Cooking time: 15 minutes
♥ v

2 **onions**
3 cloves of **garlic**
2 **leeks**
4 tablespoons **olive oil**
a thumb-sized blob of **butter**
400g **penne**
200g **frozen peas**
juice of 1 **lemon**
Parmesan cheese to taste
sea salt and **freshly ground black pepper**

1. Peel and roughly chop the onions and garlic. Trim and slice the leeks thinly.

2. Heat the oil and butter in a pan over a medium heat. Add the onions and soften for a few minutes.

3. Add the leeks and garlic, stir, and leave over a very low heat with the lid on. Check and stir every so often to make sure the leeks aren't browning. You may need to add a few drops of water (or white wine if you have some to hand).

4. Meanwhile, put the pasta on to boil. Two minutes before it is due to be ready, stir the peas and lemon juice into the leek and onion mixture and continue to cook over a medium heat until the peas are just cooked through. Season to taste.

5. Drain the pasta, return it to the pan, stir in the vegetables and serve in bowls, topped with generous handfuls of Parmesan.

 **TIPS**

o If you don't have any leeks, mushrooms are lovely. Sliced red peppers are not bad either.

Left: Pasta with Peas; Right: Spaghetti Puttanesca

SPAGHETTI PUTTANESCA

Take all the greatest-tasting store cupboard ingredients, turn them into a spaghetti sauce and this is what you get (pictured on page 120).

Feeds: 4
Preparation time: 5 minutes
Cooking time: 25 minutes
♥ DF

2 cloves of **garlic**
1 x 50g **tin of anchovies**
1 tablespoon **capers**
4 tablespoons **extra virgin olive oil**
1 **dried chilli** or 1 teaspoon **chilli powder**
1 teaspoon **dried oregano**
150g (about 2 small) **white onions**
100g drained **pitted black olives**
1 x 400g tin of **chopped tomatoes**
400g dried **spaghetti**
sea salt and **freshly ground black pepper**

1. Fill a pan with salted water and bring it to the boil.

2. Peel and finely chop the garlic, and finely chop the anchovies and capers. Heat the oil in a frying pan over a medium heat, and add the chopped ingredients. Crumble in the dried chilli and oregano, and allow to brown gently.

3. Peel and finely chop the onions and add to the pan with the olives. Coat everything well and pour in the tomatoes together with 100ml of water. Increase the heat so that the sauce is bubbling.

4. Stir regularly and cook until the tomatoes have become a darker colour.

5. Cook your spaghetti as per the packet, then drain but retain a few tablespoons of water to keep the pasta loose. Tip the pasta into the sauce and mix slowly and well, using 2 forks. Top with black pepper and Parmesan if you fancy, and serve.

 TIPS

o Add a chopped fresh chilli for extra fire.

o Clearly this will go well with other pastas besides spaghetti.

o A little chopped parsley added at the end freshens it up nicely.

FULL OF
SUN

RECIPE TESTED BY JAMES & TOBY

TUSCAN BEANS *with sage*

A vinegary bean dish, great as a side or as a summer salad (pictured on page 124).

Feeds: 4
Preparation time: 5 minutes
Cooking time: 20 minutes
♥ ✓ WF DF GF

2 cloves of **garlic**
½ an **onion**
3 tablespoons **olive oil**
4 **anchovy** fillets
30g **fresh sage**
50ml **red wine vinegar**
1 x 410g tin of **borlotti beans**
sea salt and **freshly ground black pepper**

1. Peel the garlic, crush it and chop roughly. Peel the onion and slice roughly. Fry both gently in the olive oil.

2. Chop the anchovies and sage roughly, add to the pan with the vinegar and 100ml of water, and simmer gently for 10 minutes.

3. Drain the beans, add them to the pan and cook for a further 10 minutes. Season.

TIPS

○ To make this a little more indulgent and creamy, add a blob of butter just before serving.

○ Add chopped fresh parsley at the end for some colour.

This dish was inspired by a recipe in *Beaneaters & Bread Soup* by Lori de Mori and Jason Lowe. Jason takes the photographs for our restaurant menu boards and is a force of nature, with wild red hair and an elemental passion for food. The original *fabioli al fiasco* – literally 'beans in a flask' – is made in a glass wine flask stopped with a wad of flax. The whole thing is left in the embers of a fire overnight. Not a particularly safe procedure, and one which Jason surmises might have led to our current usage of the word 'fiasco'.
Henry

FRIENDS & FAMILY
RECIPES

*The original 'fabioli al fiasco' – beans in a flask.
Photograph by Jason Lowe.*

MIMA'S GREEK-ISH BUTTER BEANS

Cheap, cheesy and healthy – this dish will tide you over when the fridge is completely bare.

Feeds: 4
Preparation time: 5 minutes
Cooking time: 40 minutes
✓ WF GF V

2 tablespoons **olive oil**
2 **red onions**
4 cloves of **garlic**
2 level teaspoons **fennel seeds**
2 teaspoons **dried oregano**
2 x 400g tins of **chopped tomatoes**
2 heaped teaspoons **tomato purée**
4 x 400g tins of **butter beans**
200g **feta cheese**
sea salt and **freshly ground black pepper**

1. Heat the oil in a large pan. Peel and chop the onions and fry gently for a couple of minutes. Peel and chop the garlic, and add it to the pan with the fennel seeds and oregano. Cook over a low heat, stirring occasionally, until the mixture looks unctuous and soft.

2. Add the tinned tomatoes and tomato purée, and leave to simmer for 20 minutes. Add the drained beans and continue to simmer for a further 10 minutes. Season.

3. Crumble most of the feta into the stew, stir well, then divide between bowls and garnish with a final crumble of feta.

 **TIPS**

○ For an extra hit of protein, fry or poach an egg and slap it on top.

Mima in Oxford, 1978

I made this up after returning home from a holiday in Greece, craving some permutation of tomato sauce with feta cheese. It is totally inauthentic, but I love it.
Mima

FRIENDS & FAMILY RECIPES

Mima's Greek-ish Butter Beans (above)

Tuscan Beans with Sage (below)

Anchovies and cream

Melt the anchovies in a little oil until they break up then mix in the cream and plenty of pepper

Butter, pepper and herbs

Chop the herbs finely and turn everything into the hot pasta

Garlic breadcrumbs

Fry the breadcrumbs in some olive oil with finely chopped garlic, salt and pepper

Blue cheese

Simply crumble over the hot pasta with a little butter and pepper

Pecans, parsley, basil and chilli

Warm some olive oil gently in a pan. Chop everything finely, drop into the olive oil, stir briefly then turn into the pasta

Almonds and garlic

Finely chop the garlic and melt gently in some butter. Turn through pasta. Season. Add the almonds on top.

CAPER & ANCHOVY MIRACLE SAUCE

There is almost nothing in this world of ours that won't be improved through the addition of this store cupboard classic.

Use it to:

1. Spoon over cooked green vegetables or boiled potatoes.

2. Drizzle over grilled or poached meat and fish.

3. Dress thin slices of grilled pumpkin or butternut squash.

4. Top mashed hard-boiled eggs on toast.

5. Dress a tomato and mozzarella salad.

6. And much, much more.

Makes: 250ml
Preparation time: 4 minutes
Cooking time: 0 minutes
✓ WF DF GF

8 **anchovy fillets**
200ml **extra virgin olive oil**
3 tablespoons **capers**
1 tablespoon fresh **lemon juice**
a large handful of chopped **fresh flat-leaf parsley**
freshly ground black pepper

1. Finely chop the anchovies and put them into a pan over a medium heat with half the oil. They will dissolve (this will take about 3 minutes). Take them off the heat.

2. Finely chop the capers and add them to the pan with the rest of the olive oil and the lemon juice. Stir.

3. Season with pepper (you shouldn't need any salt) and add the chopped parsley.

 TIPS

○ If you have no lemon juice, you can use white wine vinegar.

○ If you want to add a little punch, finely chop 2 cloves of garlic and add them to the pan halfway through heating the anchovies.

○ The trick of dissolving anchovies like this also works as a good base for other savoury or cream sauces.

SUMMER SPEED

Summer is too hot to spend time sweating in the kitchen – and if it isn't too hot, it's too short.

So whether you like to spend these precious hours clocking up laps at the lido, freaking out at a festival or simply sinking into a deckchair with a good book, these recipes are designed to give you the time to do it.

BARBECUES

A magic word. Like Christmas. Or rebate.

A barbecue is a momentary holiday. If you are throwing one, you really want to be drinking, relaxing and talking – not sweating over the coals. So it's a good idea to consider our friend Richard's advice: 'the main thing is to keep the main thing the main thing'. Cook one thing – whether it is a butterflied leg of lamb, a chicken or a couple of squid – and serve it with a salad you made earlier. That way you should have plenty of time to sit back and enjoy your holiday.

Mitch catching his first mackerel in Portmelon, Cornwall, 1974

MITCH'S BARBECUED SQUID
with chilli & peppers

Smoky marinated squid, very sweet and very summery.

This is an adaptation of a dish I first ate in a small but world-class restaurant in Dartmouth, Devon, called the Seahorse. The squid had been freshly plucked that day from the bay that was visible from the window. If you ever get the chance, I urge you to go there. The chef-proprietor, Mitch Tonks, is a master. If you can't make the trip, this recipe isn't a bad alternative. *Henry*

Feeds: 4
Preparation time: 5 minutes
Cooking time: 10 minutes
♥ ✓ WF DF GF

1 red **pepper**
1 **fresh red chilli**
1 teaspoon **dried chilli flakes**
2 **bay leaves**
2 cloves of **garlic**
50ml **extra virgin olive oil**
1 teaspoon **coriander seeds**
2 **whole squid**, skins off, cleaned inside, tentacles left on – about 230g each
sea salt and **freshly ground black pepper**

YOUR ORDER NUMBER
1

1. Light your barbecue with plenty of good lumpwood charcoal.

2. Put all the ingredients, except the squid, into a food processor and blend until smooth.

3. Pour into a bowl and add the squid, mixing to ensure that it is all covered by the marinade. Leave the squid to marinate for as long as you like.

4. When the barbecue coals are white and well burned down, put the squid on the grill and cook for around 5–8 minutes, turning once. Baste it with extra liquid as you cook it.

5. If you have any left-over marinade, pour it into a pan and bring to the boil and serve it as a sauce.

TIPS

o You can cut chunks off the squid, or slice it into rings, and eat it with a salad and bread.

o Mitch blackens the peppers and removes their skins prior to cooking, which gives them an extra smoky flavour.

o Coat the marinated squid in breadcrumbs for crunch.

Mitch's Barbecued Squid (left); Butterflied Leg of Lamb with Mint Sauce

133

BUTTERFLIED LEG OF LAMB *with mint sauce*

If we could only barbecue one dish, this would be it. It is incredibly simple and surprisingly good (pictured on page 132).

For the Lamb

Feeds: 6–8
Preparation time: 10 minutes
Cooking time: 25–30 minutes
✓ WF DF GF

1 **leg of lamb** approximately 1.5–1.7kg, butterflied (ask your butcher to do this and get him to trim the fat – it's tasty but leads to unnecessary flare-ups on the barbecue)
sea salt and **freshly ground black pepper**

1. Light the barbecue. The heat of the grill is critical. Use a lot of good charcoal – lumpwood if possible – and wait until it has died down to lovely soft white embers. If you have good depth to the charcoal you will be able to cook on it for over an hour.

2. Fill a cup with water. Season the meat well with salt and pepper. Do not rub it with oil – it just drips into the barbecue, causing flames and burning the meat. (If you have marinated the meat beforehand, pat the oil off.)

3. Put the meat on the fire and turn it every 5 minutes or so for 25–30 minutes. If it flares up, hurl on water from your cup.

4. Take the meat off and leave it for up to 30 minutes to rest.

5. Cut it across in chunks.

For the Mint Sauce

2 large handfuls of **fresh mint leaves**
2 tablespoons **runny honey**
100ml **white wine vinegar**
sea salt

1. Wash the mint and chop it as finely as you can.

2. Put the mint into a small serving bowl and add the honey.

3. Stir it well, then add the vinegar. Season.

TIPS

○ Take your lamb out of the fridge an hour or so before cooking. It leads to more even cooking and makes it less likely that you will end up with something charred on the outside and raw on the inside.

○ This is a perfect piece of meat to marinade. You can do this well in advance. Put the meat into a large bowl with plenty of olive oil, chopped rosemary, garlic and lemon zest.

○ You can use sugar or fructose in place of honey in the mint sauce.

○ We love mint sauce sharp, to cut through the fatty lamb. If it is too sharp for you, add more honey.

Liza, Sadie, Kate and Binny, Devon 1979

THE EMPEROR OF THE BARBECUE: PORTERHOUSE STEAK
with Pierre's garlic potatoes & garlicky aioli WF GF DF

You will need to ask your butcher to prepare the Porterhouse steaks for you. Eat them with a green salad and a good bottle of red. The recipes that follow are in the order in which you need to cook them (all pictured overleaf).

Feeds: 4–6

The Potatoes

Preparation time: 5 minutes
Cooking time: 30 minutes

6 tablespoons **olive oil**
700g **new potatoes**
a large bunch of **fresh rosemary**
5 cloves of **garlic**
sea salt and **freshly ground black pepper**

1. Preheat the oven to 200°C/400°F/gas mark 6. Light your barbecue with plenty of good lumpwood charcoal.

2. Pour the oil into a large roasting tin and put it into the oven to heat up for 5 minutes while you prepare the potatoes.

3. Halve the potatoes. Roughly chop the rosemary and toss with the potatoes and the unpeeled garlic cloves. Season. Add them to the roasting tin of sizzling hot oil. Return the tin to the oven and roast for 20–25 minutes, until golden brown.

The Steak

Preparation time: 5 minutes
Cooking time: 10 minutes

2 **Porterhouse steaks**
Dijon mustard
sea salt and **freshly ground black pepper**

1. Smear your steaks liberally with Dijon mustard, salt and pepper.

2. When the charcoal is white, well burned down and not too hot, pop the steaks on for about 5 minutes on each side (depending on how rare you like them).

3. Leave the meat to rest, covered in foil, for 5–10 minutes before serving, while you get the potatoes out of the oven and make the aioli.

The Aioli

Preparation time: 5 minutes
Cooking time: 0 minutes

3 cloves of **garlic**
3 **egg yolks**
1 level tablespoon **Dijon mustard**
150ml **vegetable oil**
a squeeze of **lemon juice**
sea salt and **freshly ground black pepper**

1. Peel and roughly chop the garlic and place in a food processor with the egg yolks, mustard, salt and pepper.

2. Whizz together, then slowly drizzle in the oil while the processor is still running.

3. Check the seasoning and add a squeeze of lemon juice.

 **TIPS**

- It is critical that the barbecue is not too hot, otherwise you will produce raw steak with a charcoal crust.

- You can use T-bone steaks, which are the same cut but from further down the animal so that you get less fillet.

- Thyme, marjoram or oregano will work just as well with the potatoes if you don't like rosemary. For a warmer, smoky taste you could use paprika instead of herbs.

- This is also a great way to cook quick roast potatoes for a Sunday lunch.

- The aioli can be served with any grilled meat or fish, or simply for dipping a crust of bread into.

We ate this on a hot summer's day in our garden when a generous guest turned up with two huge slabs of meat. A Porterhouse steak is in fact two-in-one: a fillet steak and a sirloin steak still joined together by the T-bone. We lit the barbecue and Pierre threw together some aioli and potatoes. The fillet on one side was sweet and buttery and the sirloin on the other was rampant and gamey with age. Expensive but a great once-in-a-summer treat.
Henry

SPATCHCOCKED CHICKEN *with aubergines & tomatoes*

An elegant way to cook chicken on the barbecue without having to juggle loads of charring drummers.

Feeds: 4
Preparation time: 10 minutes
Cooking time: 40 minutes
✓ WF DF GF

1 medium **chicken**
4 sprigs of **fresh thyme**
juice of ½ **lemon**
1 large **aubergine**
2 tablespoons **extra virgin olive oil**
4 **tomatoes**
sea salt and **freshly ground black pepper**

1. First, light the barbecue. The heat of the grill is critical. Use a lot of good charcoal – lumpwood if possible – and wait until it has died down to lovely soft white embers. If you have good depth to the charcoal you will be able to cook on it for over an hour.

2. Spatchcock the chicken (see opposite).

3. Finely chop the thyme. Rub the chicken with salt and pepper, half the thyme and squeeze over the lemon juice. You can use oil, but this increases the risk of charring.

4. Cut the ends off the aubergine and slice lengthways into 1cm pieces. Toss in a bowl with the olive oil and the rest of the thyme. Cut the tomatoes in half and season the cut sides.

5. When the barbecue is ready, place the chicken on the grill, skin side down. Turn it every 5 minutes. Watch it for flaming – if the flames fire up, douse them with a good slosh of water. It will take about 40 minutes to cook.

6. While you are cooking the chicken, cook the tomatoes and aubergines in batches alongside it. The aubergines will take about 2 minutes on each side. The tomatoes will take about 4 minutes on each side.

TIPS

○ Serve with Green Sauce (page 141).

○ If you don't fancy spatchcocking your chicken yourself, ask your butcher to do it for you. Alternatively, you can buy them ready done in the supermarket.

○ For extra show, you can squeeze a stuffing under the skin of the bird prior to cooking. Simple combinations work well. Think garlic and tarragon, fried mushrooms and thyme, or parsley and cream cheese. For the more adventurous, lime pickle blitzed with butter in the food processor is terrific, as is grated courgette with Parmesan.

○ You can use the spatchcocking technique to reduce the time it takes to cook a roast chicken. A spatchcocked chicken will roast in a 200°C/400°F/gas mark 6 oven in only 30 minutes.

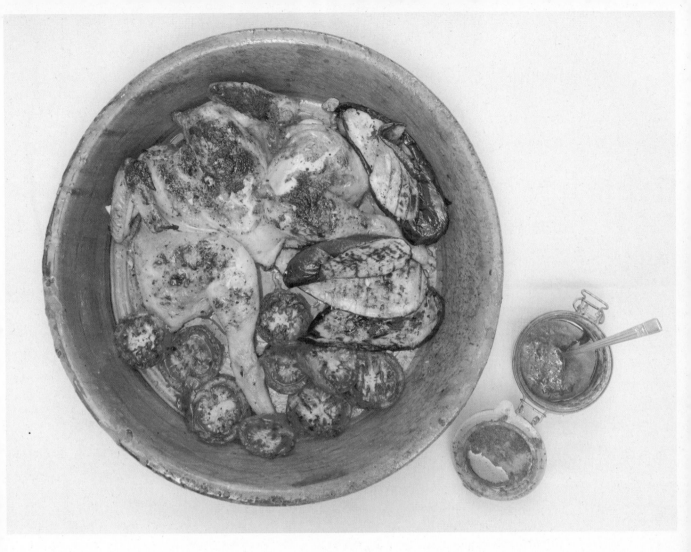

THE

JOY OF SPATCHCOCKING

1. Put the bird on a board breast-side down.
    Cut with the shears or a large knife one
    side of the backbone (classically at this
    stage you would cut down the other side
    as well and entirely remove the backbone,
    but we think this isn't necessary).

2. Pull the legs apart. Put the bird cavity
    side down and push the whole thing flat.
    (Again, traditionally you would remove
    the breastbone from inside the cavity.
    But this is not necessary either.)

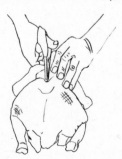

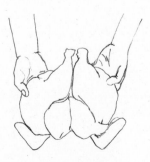

CHIMICHURRI SAUCE

An Argentinian sauce that comes to life when it hits hot meat.

Feeds: 4 (makes about 300ml)
Preparation time: 10 minutes
Cooking time: 0 minutes
♥ ✓ WF DF GF V

a large handful of **fresh flat-leaf parsley**
2 cloves of **garlic**
1 tablespoon **smoked sweet paprika**
1 tablespoon **dried oregano** or **thyme**
1 tablespoon **cayenne pepper**
150ml **extra virgin olive oil**
75ml **red wine vinegar**
sea salt and **freshly ground black pepper**

1. Wash the parsley and shake dry. Peel the garlic.

2. Put all the ingredients into a blender and whizz until smooth.

3. Season.

TIPS

o Traditionally served with beef, but it works well with lamb, too. It also works with fish that will stand up to it – for example barbecued monkfish, turbot or cod.

o Next time you are invited to a barbecue, take a big tub of this along as well as your chops. You will be very popular.

o Also good heated briefly in a pan and poured over boiled vegetables for a healthy supper.

GREEN SAUCE

A fresh, vibrant sauce that goes with almost anything.

Feeds: 4 (makes about 320ml)
Preparation time: 10 minutes
Cooking time: 0 minutes
♥ ✓ WF DF GF

a large handful of **fresh mint**
a large handful of **fresh flat-leaf parsley**
a large handful of **fresh coriander**
1 tablespoon **capers**
2 teaspoons **Dijon mustard**
4 **anchovy fillets**
200ml **extra virgin olive oil**
juice of ½ a **lemon**
sea salt and **freshly ground black pepper**

1. Put all the ingredients into a blender and whizz until smooth. It should be runny but substantial.

2. Transfer to a sealable jar and pop into the fridge.

TIPS

o Serve with any simply barbecued, grilled or roasted meat or fish – it is that versatile.

o Spoon over vegetables for a simple supper.

o You can omit the anchovies if you need to – but they do give a rich depth of flavour.

o You can use any green herbs you have to hand – basil and tarragon both work well, too.

INDIAN BARBECUE SAUCE

An easy barbecue sauce that can double as a marinade.

Feeds: 4 (makes about 280ml)
Preparation time: 5 minutes
Cooking time: 0 minutes
♥ ✓ WF GF V

250g **natural yoghurt**
3 teaspoons good **tikka masala paste**
½ a **lemon**
a large handful of **fresh coriander**

1. Put the yoghurt into a bowl and stir in the tikka masala paste.

2. Add lemon juice and chopped coriander to taste.

TIPS

o Great with lamb, chicken or beef.

o Dip cooked meat into this sauce, or use it to marinate meat before putting it on the barbecue.

FULL OF
SUN

141

STUFFED PICNIC COB LOAF

A great picnic dish – your imagination is the only thing limiting what can go inside it.

Feeds: 8
Preparation time: 10 minutes
Cooking time: 0 minutes

1 medium-sized **cob loaf**
½ jar of **pesto**
200–300g tub of **cream cheese**
100–200g **salami**
1 large **red pepper**
100g **sun-blush tomatoes**
100g **Parma ham**
large handful of **fresh spinach leaves**
sea salt and **freshly ground black pepper**

1. Cut the top off the loaf and scrape out the bread inside, leaving the crusty shell. Reserve the top.

2. Spread the inside of the loaf with a thin layer of pesto.

3. Start layering up the loaf with cream cheese, salami slices, thin slices of red pepper, tomatoes, Parma ham and spinach, sprinkling with salt and pepper as you go along, and repeating the layers until the loaf is full. Cover with clingfilm and put something heavy on top to weight it down.

4. Leave in the fridge for at least 4 hours.

5. Put the top back on and either serve cold or pop into a hot oven for 5 minutes to crisp it up – wrap it in foil and off you go. To serve, slice like a cake.

TIPS

o You can make this 12 hours before you leave for your picnic.

o Just about anything can be layered in the loaf:

o **Veggie option:** with roasted butternut squash, chargrilled courgettes, roasted red peppers, roasted mushrooms, spinach leaves, pesto and Parmesan shavings.

o **Fish option:** with smoked salmon, rocket leaves, sun-blush tomatoes, lettuce, lemon juice, black pepper, crème fraîche.

o **Meat option:** with chicken, mayonnaise, lettuce, tomatoes and bacon.

o You can use all the antipasti from the chilled shelf – artichoke hearts in oil, chargrilled peppers and courgettes, marinated mushrooms, anchovies, etc. The world is your oyster.

Nat, Daisy, Eleanor, Natasha, Clemmie, Mabel, Wilf, George & Arthur, 2009

I saw something similar to this recipe in an Australian housekeeping magazine years ago. We now try and spend as much time in north Norfolk (my old stomping ground), as possible and often take our leaky little day boat out at Brancaster. Fried eggs and bacon cooked on the Calor gas for breakfast and then the cob loaf for lunch, which I made the night before. Magical! *Apple*

A comely collection of colourful coolers

CUCUMBER COOLER

This might just be the most beautiful-looking drink in the world, and it's refreshing too.

Makes 2 litres (before ice)
♥ ✓ WF DF GF V

1 **cucumber**
1 **lime**
1.5 litres **cold water**

1. Peel the cucumber, discarding the peel. Then, still using the peeler, keep peeling the flesh into long ribbons, turning it as you go. Drop the cucumber ribbons straight into your favourite jug, and keep making more until you get to the seeds.

2. Squeeze in the juice of the lime, and add the water and lots of ice.

MELON FIZZ

Makes 1.4 litres
♥ ✓ WF DF GF V

1 ripe **cantaloupe melon**
juice of 2 **limes**
1 litre **cold fizzy water**

1. Peel the melon and remove the seeds. Chop the flesh and blend it in a food processor with the juice of 1 lime.

2. Pour through a sieve or fine strainer, into a wide-necked jug or bowl, squeezing as much of the juice through as you can.

3. Top up with fizzy water and serve.

SPARKLING STRAWBERRY COOLER

Makes 1.4 litres
♥ ✓ WF DF GF V

300g **strawberries**
6 **fresh mint leaves**
juice of **1 lemon**
2 tablespoons **honey**
1 litre **cold sparkling water**

1. Whizz everything except the water in a blender.

2. Add ice to the blender if you wish.

3. Transfer to a jug and mix in the sparkling water, and serve.

From left: Sparkling Strawberry Cooler; Cucumber Cooler; Melon Fizz

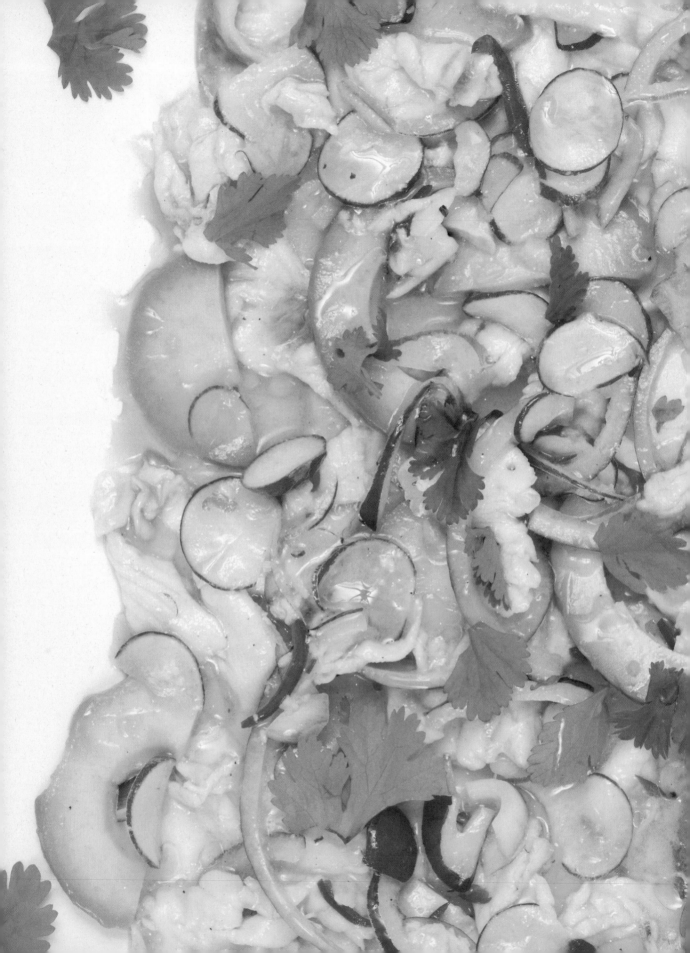

RAW FOOD

SOME OF THE GREAT SUMMER DISHES
REQUIRE NO COOKING AT ALL

Ceviche (recipe on page 148)

CEVICHE

A simple, stunning and super-fresh dish for a hot summer's day. The lemon juice 'cooks' the fish delicately. Eat with a glass of white wine so cold there's a kind of mist on the side of the glass.

Feeds: 4 (as a starter or light lunch)
Preparation time: 15 minutes
Cooking time: 0 minutes

♥ ✓ WF GF DF

½ a **fresh red chilli**
½ a **red onion**
a handful of **radishes** (the bigger each radish the better)
250g of **sea bass fillet** (equivalent to a 600g bass), boned and skinned
juice of 1 **lemon**
3 tablespoons **extra virgin olive oil**
1 **avocado**
a small bunch of **fresh coriander**
sea salt & **freshly ground black pepper**

1. Deseed and slice the chilli into fine strips and peel and slice the red onion as fine as you can manage. Slice the radishes very thinly.

2. Finely slice the sea bass into strips and put it in a bowl with the chilli, onion and radishes together with the lemon juice and olive oil.

3. Season well with salt and pepper – this is the most important step with ceviche. You have a very simple balance of flavours, so take time to get the seasoning just right. Add more chilli and lemon juice if necessary.

4. Leave for 10 minutes – and no more (less if you like it a little sushi-style). If you leave it for too long the fish will 'overcook'.

5. Peel the avocado and cut in half, remove the stone and slice each half into delicate half moons. Arrange the fish mixture on a large plate, pour over any remaining lemon marinade and drizzle with a little extra olive oil. Scatter over the coriander leaves and serve.

 TIPS

o In Peru this is a national dish. They often eat it as a simple lunch – *almuerzo* – with baked sweet potato. The orange colour and sweet taste of the potato make a wonderful switch for the avocado in this recipe.

o Ceviche is one of those dishes you can experiment with. Try lime juice instead of lemon. Change the fish – use scallops, raw prawns, or salmon. Use pieces of grilled corn on the cob from the barbecue instead of avocado.

o Make it your own (see page 151).

CARPACCIO WITH PARMESAN CRISP

Very quick, much easier than people think, and super-impressive (pictured on page 150).

Feeds: 4
Preparation time: 10 minutes
Cooking time: 5 minutes

✓ WF GF

½ teaspoon **coriander seeds**
½ teaspoon **cumin seeds**
½ teaspoon **sea salt**
½ teaspoon **freshly ground black pepper**
500g **fillet** or **sirloin steak** (a tender good-quality one)
2 tablespoons **extra virgin olive oil**
a lime-sized lump of **Parmesan cheese**
1 tablespoon **crème fraîche** or **fromage frais**
a handful of **rocket leaves**
1 tablespoon **balsamic vinegar**

1. Grind the spices, salt and pepper together and rub well into the steak. Sear the outside of the meat in a hot pan for 1 minute with 1 tablespoon of the olive oil. Remove it from the pan, let it cool then wrap it in clingfilm and put into the fridge.

2. Grate the Parmesan super-fine and sprinkle it in an even layer on to a hot non-stick pan. It will bubble and go slightly golden. Slide it off with a spatula and leave on a piece of kitchen paper. As it cools, it will crisp up.

3. Slice the meat finely and arrange it on a plate with blobs of crème fraîche. Sprinkle the rocket on top, and drizzle with the balsamic vinegar and the remaining olive oil. Season. Break the Parmesan crisp into pieces and scatter on top.

 TIPS

o You can place the steak under clingfilm after searing and slicing, and whack it with a rolling pin if you want it super-fine. We never bother, but you can if you want to.

o This goes brilliantly with Anchovy & Caper Miracle Sauce (recipe on page 128).

o For variations on this theme, see page 151.

RECIPE TESTED BY OLI

BIG AND STRONG

LEON

35-36 GREAT MARLBOROUGH STREET LONDON W1F 7JE

SIX WAYS WITH CEVICHE

A great ceviche requires a sharp marinated fishy element and a sweet element (the bass and avocado respectively in the main recipe on page 148). You can use the same technique to make any number of variations. These are some that we have tried in the past. Keep the onion, chilli, oil and coriander and replace the fish, radish and avocado with the listed ingredients.

English:
Finely sliced scallops and pea shoots.

West Indian:
Finely sliced large, raw prawns with mango and avocado.

Peruvian:
Sea bass with small chunks of roasted sweet potato.

Scottish:
Wild salmon and very finely sliced fennel.

Vegetarian:
Courgettes, sliced thinly into tongues using a peeler.

AND AN ADDED BONUS…

Leche de tigre (tiger's milk):
Mix the liquid that runs off the ceviche with ice-cold vodka. A great aperitif or hangover cure.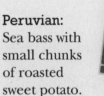

SIX WAYS WITH CARPACCIO

Once you have your basic carpaccio recipe down pat, you can play with all sorts of variations for the toppers. Our favourites include:

Classic:
Drizzled with a mustardy dressing (the one for the leek vinaigrette on page 64 works really well).

British:
Little roast beetroots with horseradish cream and watercress.

Fusion:
Finely sliced chillies and a drizzle of soy sauce.

Continental:
Capers, olive oil and baby spinach leaves.

Summer:
Finely shaved fennel in a light lemon and olive oil dressing.

Posh:
Parmesan shavings, olive oil and finely sliced black truffle.

Left: Carpaccio with Parmesan Crisp

Courgette Cannelloni

Gabriela's Raw Feast

It's always interesting to dip one's toes into the wilder shores of culinary fashion. So when our friend Gabriela – a holistic health consultant who lived for years in New York and LA – offered to cook us an entirely 'raw' feast, curiosity overcame us.

The raw food movement is about much more than celery sticks. Raw evangelists eat only uncooked, unprocessed, unpasteurized and usually organic food, which they believe is closer to our natural diet. By eliminating cooked food, they claim their bodies benefit from the vitamins, minerals and enzymes that get destroyed in the cooking process, and thereby gain health and vitality.

The constraints of raw food can encourage amazing creativity: Gabriela introduced us, for instance, to delicious 'dehydrated crackers' and rich creamy 'casheez' – a substitute for cream cheese made from soaked and ground cashew nuts. But the dishes opposite are straightforward enough for anyone to try.

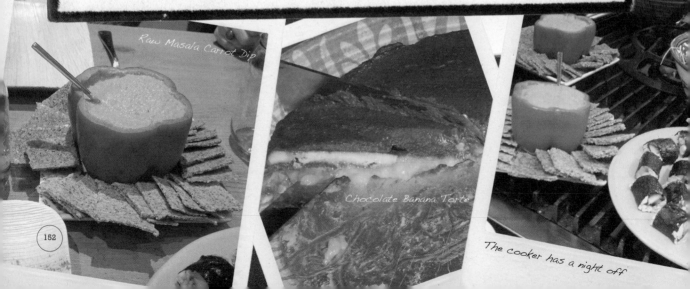
Raw Masala Carrot Dip

Chocolate Banana Torte

The cooker has a night off

Gabriela, preparing our feast

Gabriela Garay
Holistic Health Services
gabriela@thepickyfoodie.com

Raw Food Feast Menu

Gabriela's Green Smoothie
(see page 41)

......

Raw Masala Carrot Dip
(with three kinds of dehydrated crackers:
onion, rosemary and cheesy hazelnut)

......

Vegan Mushroom Sushi

......

Courgette Cannelloni with Casheez
in a Fresh Tomato and Herb Sauce

......

Chocolate Banana Torte

Vegan sushi

Dipping sauce for sushi rolls

RAW MASALA CARROT DIP

Makes: 1 litre
Preparation time: 10 minutes
Cooking time: 0 minutes
♥ ✓ WF DF GF V

750g **carrots**
250ml raw **tahini**
juice of 1 **lemon**
juice of 1 **orange**
1 teaspoon **garam masala**
3 teaspoons **ground cumin**
½ a small **onion**
a 2.5cm piece of **fresh ginger**
3 **pitted dates**
80ml **extra virgin olive oil**
a large handful of **fresh coriander leaves**
sea salt and **freshly ground black pepper**

1. Wash the carrots, peel and cut into large chunks. Put into a food processor with 240ml of water and whizz until smooth.

2. Add the tahini, lemon juice, orange juice, garam masala, cumin and a pinch of salt and whizz until smooth. Peel the onion and ginger then add them and the dates one ingredient at a time and whizz again until smooth.

3. Add the oil, processing as you go, and adding up to 80ml of water if you think it needs it. Season.

4. Add the coriander leaves, reserving a few, and whizz one more time.

5. Chop the reserved coriander leaves and use as a garnish.

6. Serve with crackers or chunks of vegetables for dipping.

 TIPS

○ If you have a high-quality blender you can make a really smooth final texture by transferring the mixture to the blender for a final whizz before serving.

○ If you can't find raw tahini, use normal tahini found in supermarkets and health stores.

RAW CHOCOLATE BANANA TORTE

It is important to start by making the base layer so that it has time to set in the freezer.

Feeds: 10
Preparation time: 20 minutes
Cooking time: 0 minutes
♥ ✓ WF DF GF V

100g whole **almonds**
6 **pitted dates**
50g **sunflower seeds**
a pinch of **salt**
60ml melted **coconut oil**
4 **bananas**
2 **avocados**
2 tablespoons **tahini**
6 tablespoons **cacao powder**
½ teaspoon **vanilla powder**
2–4 teaspoons **honey**, depending on how sweet you like it

1. Combine the almonds, dates, sunflower seeds and salt in a food processor. Melt the coconut oil in a bain-marie to avoid overheating. Once the oil has liquefied, pour it into the food processor while the engine is running. The mixture should end up as more or less one uniform ball.

2. Divide into 2 parts, one larger (about ¾), one smaller (about ¼), and put the smaller one aside. Press the larger part into a 20cm loose-bottomed cake tin with the base of your palm until it is about 5mm thick. Put it into the freezer to set while you prepare the other layers.

3. Peel the bananas, mash up 2 and cut the remaining 2 into even slices.

4. Peel the avocados and discard the stone. Place the flesh in a food processor with the tahini and blend well. Add the cacao and vanilla powder, then the honey. At the very end, dilute ever so slightly with a little water.

5. Remove the bottom layer of the torte from the freezer and cover it with the mashed bananas. At this point, roll out the second, smaller chunk of base layer dough until it is about as thick as a pancake and gently place on top of the mashed bananas.

6. Gently arrange the sliced bananas over the entire surface.

7. Cover with the avocado layer and place in the fridge until you are ready to serve it.

 TIPS

o   For a sweeter torte, use riper bananas. If you cannot find vanilla powder, use vanilla extract.

o   Watch people's faces carefully when you tell them (after they have eaten it) that it contains avocado.

SUMMER SALADS

A barbecue needs a salad as surely as Romeo needed Juliet.

These are four of our favourite simple barbecue salads, and a collection of punchy dressings.

GREEN SUNSHINE SALAD

This is a popular side dish in the restaurants – we wanted to create something simple and fresh, and the mint gives it real zing.

Feeds: 4 (as a generous side)
Preparation time: 10 minutes
Cooking time: 5 minutes
♥ ✓ WF DF GF V

200g **green beans**
400g **frozen peas**
400g **frozen edamame beans**
a large handful of **fresh mint**
125ml **Leon House Dressing** (recipe on page 163)

1. Top the green beans and chop them in half. Cook them briefly in boiling water, then refresh them in a bowl of cold water.

2. Defrost the peas and the edamame beans.

3. Roughly chop the mint.

4. Drain the green beans and combine all the ingredients together.

TIPS

o You can use any mix of green beans for this salad – frozen broad beans and runner beans both work a treat if you can't get hold of edamame beans.

THIRTIETH BIRTHDAY PEA SALAD

Feeds: 4
Preparation time: 5 minutes
Cooking time: 10 minutes
♥ ✓ WF DF GF V

1 **red pepper**
2.5cm piece of **fresh ginger**
2 cloves of **garlic**
6 **spring onions**
2 tablespoons **extra virgin olive oil**
1 teaspoon **black mustard seeds**
1 teaspoon **red wine vinegar**
250g **frozen peas**
a small handful of **fresh coriander**, washed
sea salt and **freshly ground black pepper**

I first made this salad at my joint 30th birthday party with my friends Simon and Roly. We made it for about 150 people, dressing it by tossing it in (clean) black bin liners – a useful trick. *Henry*

1. Halve and deseed the pepper, and cut into slices. Peel and grate the ginger and garlic. Trim the spring onions and cut on the diagonal into long thin strips.

2. Heat the olive oil in a saucepan over a medium heat and fry the mustard seeds until they pop. Swirl in the garlic and ginger.

3. Add the pepper, stirring well until it picks up some colour. Add the spring onions and the vinegar. It will sizzle a bit.

4. Throw in the peas with a tiny splash of water and leave to defrost and warm up, stirring occasionally. You are not looking to cook them, just to get them up to room temperature.

5. Remove from the heat. Season and add the chopped coriander.

WARM ANCHOVY, GARLIC & POTATO SALAD

Pouring a dressing on to warm potatoes has a wonderful effect, as the potatoes soften and absorb the flavours. This dish is very moreish.

Feeds: 4
Preparation time: 5 minutes
Cooking time: 20 minutes
♥ WF GF DF

800g **new potatoes**
3 cloves of **garlic**
2 tablespoons **white wine vinegar**
1 x 50g tin **anchovy fillets**
100ml **extra virgin olive oil**
1 tablespoon finely chopped **fresh chives**
sea salt and **freshly ground black pepper**

1. Chop the potatoes in half and boil them, covered, in a large pan of salted water until tender.

2. Put the garlic, vinegar and anchovies into a blender and whizz to form a paste. With the blender running, drizzle in the extra virgin olive oil. Season.

3. Drain the potatoes and pour the dressing over them, tossing them well.

4. Allow to cool for 3 minutes, then toss again. Sprinkle with the chopped chives and serve.

 TIPS

○ It is a good idea to cut the potatoes in half with a fork once cooked, so that they are roughed up and absorb the anchovy dressing.

○ You can use parsley in the place of chives.

○ If you can't get hold of new potatoes, any waxy potatoes will do. If you use bigger ones, peel them and chop them into chunks.

○ Great as a side salad at a barbecue. Make it in the morning and serve it later at room temperature.

Leon, Eastern Mediterranean, 1959

Above:
Warm Anchovy, Garlic & Potato Salad
Below: Thirtieth Birthday Salad

Our favourite trick for creating a sumptuous green salad (other than a great salad dressing – see page 163) is to chop lots of herbs finely and toss them in among the leaves.

QUICK GREEN SALAD

Leafy herbs all work: dill, parsley, sage, coriander, chives, oregano, marjoram and mint. Add as many different types as you like to a single salad for a flavour explosion.

FOUR SIMPLE DRESSINGS

1

2

3

4

1 TAPENADE DRESSING

Best used to dress strong-flavoured salad leaves or cooked greens.

Makes 100ml   Preparation time: 3 minutes   Cooking time: 0 minutes   ♥ ✓ WF DF GF (V if you use anchovy-free tapenade)

2 tablespoons **tapenade**
1 tablespoon **sherry vinegar**
5 tablespoons **extra virgin olive oil**
sea salt and **freshly ground black pepper**

1. Put all the ingredients into a jam jar.
2. Shake well, and check the seasoning.

2 LEON HOUSE DRESSING

Gives a real punch to old fashioned lettuce leaves. Keeps well in the fridge.

Makes 450ml   Preparation time: 3 minutes   Cooking time: 0 minutes   ♥ ✓ WF DF GF V

2 tablespoons **Dijon mustard**
80ml **white wine vinegar**
350ml **rapeseed oil**
sea salt and **freshly ground black pepper**

1. Blend the mustard and vinegar in a blender.
2. Keeping the blender running, slowly add the rapeseed oil until you have a fully emulsified dressing.
3. Season carefully.

3 BALSAMIC DRESSING

Best for simple green salads with lots of chopped herbs in them.

Makes 75ml   Preparation time: 3 minutes   Cooking time: 0 minutes   ♥ ✓ WF DF GF V

2 tablespoons **balsamic vinegar**
  (use a nice syrupy aged one if you can)
6 tablespoons **extra virgin olive oil**
  (a good one really makes a difference)
sea salt and **freshly ground black pepper**

1. Put the ingredients straight on to the salad.
2. Grind over lots of black pepper and add a generous amount of salt.
3. Toss with vigour.

4 ORIENTAL DRESSING

Best on shredded vegetables – for example, grated carrot and courgette or finely shredded Chinese cabbage.

Makes 75ml   Preparation time: 8 minutes   Cooking time: 0 minutes   ♥ ✓ WF DF GF V

1 fat clove of **garlic**
1cm piece of **fresh ginger**
1 **spring onion**
½ a **fresh red chilli**
1 tablespoon **fish sauce**
juice of ½ a **lime**
3 tablespoons **peanut oil** or
  other flavourless oil
1 tablespoon **toasted sesame oil**

1. In a small clean jar with a lid, use your finest grater to grate the garlic and ginger into the jar.
2. Finely slice the spring onion and deseed and finely chop the chilli. Add to the jar.
3. Measure in the fish sauce and lime juice and add the oils. Screw on the lid and shake well.

TIPS

○ You can add a little honey if you like your dressing sweet.

Three grown-up iced lollies to cool you down on a hot summer's day.

Each recipe makes lollies for 6

STRAWBERRY LOLLY

Preparation time: 10 minutes
Freezing time: Overnight
(minimum 2½ hours)
♥ ✓ WF DF GF V

600g **strawberries,** hulled
3 level teaspoons **fructose**
1 tablespoon **vodka**

1. Put the strawberries, fructose and vodka into a blender and blend until smooth.

2. Divide equally between lolly moulds and push in the sticks (or cut-off straws).

3. Put in the freezer until firm.

MANGO LOLLY

♥ ✓ WF DF GF V

2kg **mango flesh**
3 level teaspoons **fructose**
1 tablespoon **vodka**

1. Put the mango, fructose and vodka into a blender and blend until smooth.

2. Divide equally between lolly moulds and push in the sticks (or cut-off straws).

3. Put in the freezer until firm.

BAILEYS LOLLY

✓ WF GF V

500ml **double cream**
3 level teaspoons **fructose**
3 tablespoons **Baileys**

1. Put the cream, fructose and Baileys into a blender and blend until smooth.

2. Divide equally between lolly moulds and push in the sticks (or cut-off straws).

3. Put in the freezer until firm.

TIPS

o The vodka brings out the flavour of the fruit. You can leave the alcohol out if you want to avoid sedating your children.

o Create a rocket ship (see opposite) – this is tricky but rewarding. Freeze each of these ices in individual layers one after the other. Then drizzle a little melted chocolate on top (make sure the lolly is *really* cold first), and sprinkle on some space dust or sherbet. Cool on a sheet of greaseproof paper in the freezer.

Rocket ship lolly. Background drawing by Madelaine Cooper.

FABULOUS
ICED LOLLIES

HATTIE AND APPLE'S GUIDE TO COOKING WITH KIDS

CHICKEN NUGGETS

Feeds: 4 children
Preparation time: 10 minutes
Cooking time: 15 minutes
♥ ✓ DF

2 **chicken breasts** or **boneless thighs**
1 **egg**
2 handfuls of **breadcrumbs**
½ tablespoon **olive oil**

1. Preheat the oven to 180°C/350°F/gas mark 4.

2. Cut the chicken into nugget-sized pieces.

3. Crack the egg into a bowl and whisk with a fork. Put the breadcrumbs on a plate. Dip the chicken pieces into the beaten egg and roll in the breadcrumbs.

4. Line a baking tray with foil or baking parchment, and arrange the chicken pieces on it. Sprinkle with the oil.

5. Place into the oven for about 15 minutes, or until the chicken coating is lightly brown and the chicken cooked through.

TIPS

○ Use brown grainy breadcrumbs, or a mix of breadcrumbs and crushed ready-salted crisps, for extra crunch.

OVEN CHIPS

All sensible people, adults or children, like a bowl of chips every now and then, so make them the healthy way at home.

Feeds: 4 children
Preparation time: 5 minutes
Cooking time: 30 minutes
♥ WF DF GF V

500g **potatoes**, any kind
3 tablespoons **olive oil** or **vegetable oil**
sea salt and **freshly ground black pepper**

1. Preheat the oven to 180°C/350°F/gas mark 4.

2. Wash the potatoes under the tap and remove any gnarly bits. Leaving the skins on, cut the potatoes into thin chips.

3. Put the chips into an oven dish, cover with the oil, season and and toss well.

4. Place the dish in the oven and cook for 30 minutes, or until the chips are crisp.

5. Do not serve the chips until they have cooled down sufficiently for small mouths!

TIPS

○ Serve with homemade chicken nuggets, fish fingers, or dip into hummus.

○ Try different seasonings such as chopped thyme, ground allspice or garam masala.

Oven chips in the bowl, fish fingers and chicken nuggets on the plate

FRESH FISH FINGERS

Forget buying fish fingers: even the posh luxury ones you can get nowadays won't taste as good as if you make them yourself. Make a double batch and freeze the rest.

Makes: 25 mini fish fingers
Preparation time: 15 minutes
Cooking time: 10 minutes

♥ ✓

300g **fish** (I use salmon fillet)
1 large **egg**
40g **flour**
100g **breadcrumbs**
grated **Parmesan cheese** – optional
sea salt and **freshly ground pepper** – optional
2 tablespoons **olive oil** or **rapeseed oil**

1. Check your fish carefully for bones.

2. With a sharp knife cut the fish into fish finger shapes, about 1cm wide and 3cm long.

3. Crack the egg into a clean bowl, and whisk lightly. Put the flour into another bowl, and the breadcrumbs into a third bowl. Add Parmesan and seasoning to the flour if you wish.

4. Working in batches, coat the fish first in the flour, then dip in the egg and finally roll in the breadcrumbs.

5. Heat the oil in a non-stick frying pan and gently fry the fish fingers until golden.

6. Serve when cool enough to eat.

 TIPS

o   You can use any fish you like – I like salmon. And if you prefer not to use white flour, feel free to use any kind.

ARTHUR'S FAVOURITE DUCK & LETTUCE WRAPS

A healthy and fun dish for the children to help make.

Feeds: 4 children
Preparation time: 5 minutes
Cooking time: 25 minutes

WF DF GF

1 **cucumber**
2 **little gem lettuces**
1 **duck breast**
olive oil
a jar of **plum sauce**
sea salt and **freshly ground pepper**

1. Preheat the oven to 190°C/375°F/gas mark 5. Cut the cucumber into batons and put into a bowl. Separate the lettuce leaves and put into a second bowl.

2. Season the duck breast and add a dash of olive oil and roast for about 25 minutes, until the skin is crispy. Separate the cooked meat into little bits, using 2 forks.

3. Get the children to make parcels, wrapping the duck and cucumber in the lettuce leaves, and serve the plum sauce on the side in a small bowl.

GEORGE PICKARD'S CHEESE & HAM MUFFINS

A great snack for when you get back from school instead of sugary biscuits.

Makes: 12 Preparation time: 15 minutes Cooking time: 20 minutes	6 slices of **ham** 190g **Cheddar cheese** 75g **butter** 1 **egg** 250ml **milk** 300g **self-raising flour** ½ teaspoon **paprika** a pinch of **sea salt**

1. Preheat the oven to 190°C/375°F/gas mark 5. Lightly grease a muffin tin.

2. Cut the ham into 1cm chunks, and grate the Cheddar or chop it roughly. Cut the butter into pieces. Beat the egg in a bowl with the milk.

3. Sieve the flour, paprika and salt into a large mixing bowl, and rub the butter into the flour until it looks like breadcrumbs.

4. Add the ham and cheese, then pour in the egg and milk mixture and mix thoroughly.

5. Spoon into the muffin tin and cook in the oven for 20 minutes.

6. Place on a wire rack to cool.

George loves cooking and learnt this recipe at school – I often find him in the kitchen making these on his own. Sadly they don't last very long, as they are delicious! *Apple*

FRIENDS & FAMILY RECIPES

George, High House Farm 2007

LAMB & APRICOT BALLS

A quick and easy supper. Delicious with mashed sweet potatoes.

Makes: about 25 meatballs
Preparation time: 15 minutes
Cooking time: 10–15 minutes
✓ WF DF GF

1 **onion**
50g **dried apricots**
3 tablespoons **olive oil**
500g **minced lamb**
1 small **egg**
sea salt and **freshly ground black pepper** – optional

1. Peel the onion and put into a food processor with the apricots. Blitz until they are both very finely chopped. If you don't have a food processor, chop them very finely by hand.

2. Heat 1 tablespoon of the olive oil in a small frying pan. Add the onions and apricots and cook gently for 10–15 minutes, stirring occasionally to make sure they don't burn.

3. Put the minced lamb into a large bowl, add the egg and mix with your hands. Add the onions and apricots to the lamb, and mix again. If you wish to add salt and pepper do this now.

4. With clean wet hands roll the lamb mixture into small balls, and set them aside on a plate.

5. Heat the rest of the olive oil in a pan, and gently fry the lamb balls until golden and cooked through. This should take about 10 minutes. Let them cool down a little before serving to children.

TIPS

o You can add herbs and very finely chopped spinach to the lamb mixture if you want to sneak in some veg.

o Depending on the children, and how exotic their palate is, add ground cumin and cinnamon for an extra twist.

o If you do not want to fry these, you can oven bake them at 180°C/350°F/gas mark 4 for about 15 minutes.

o Perfect for the freezer and can even be cooked from frozen.

Ned reading the papers, summer 2009

FRIENDS & FAMILY
RECIPES

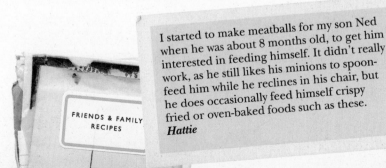

I started to make meatballs for my son Ned when he was about 8 months old, to get him interested in feeding himself. It didn't really work, as he still likes his minions to spoon-feed him while he reclines in his chair, but he does occasionally feed himself crispy fried or oven-baked foods such as these.
Hattie

TEATIME &

ELEVENSES

Tea and elevenses:
two great British institutions.
Yet on busy days, you might not even notice yourself
indulging in one or another. Too easily, snacking becomes
something you do unthinkingly to stop yourself
falling asleep at your desk.

Done right, however, a snack is more than just a small energy
boost. It can be a real treat, a shared ritual with friends,
a moment of escapism.

MUM'S CHOCOLATE & FRUIT BISCUIT CAKE

An old-fashioned no-cook way to make a rich and crunchy cake; it can be kept in a tin in the fridge for weeks if in the unlikely event that you don't eat it all straight away.

Feeds: 10–12
Preparation time: 10 minutes
Cooking time: 10 minutes

 v

175g **butter**
3 tablespoons **clear honey**
225g **dark chocolate**
175g **ginger biscuits**
175g **rich tea biscuits**
80g soft **dried apricots**
4 **dried figs**
70g large **seedless raisins**
zest and juice of 1 **orange**
a dusting of **icing sugar**

1. Butter a deep 20–22cm diameter cake tin (or any shaped tin will do) but not one with a loose base.

2. Put the butter, honey and broken-up chocolate into a fairly large pan over a low heat and stir until smoothly melted together.

3. Crush the ginger and rich tea biscuits roughly, either briefly in a food processor or with a rolling pin.

4. Chop the apricots and figs into small pieces and stir into the melted chocolate mixture, along with the raisins, crushed biscuits, orange zest and juice. Mix thoroughly together, then turn into the prepared cake tin and spread level.

5. Chill in the fridge until set, then dip the tin briefly in very hot water and turn out on to a serving plate. Leave at room temperature for at least 30 minutes before eating, then sprinkle the top with icing sugar through a fine sieve and cut into thin slices with a sharp knife.

TIPS

- Don't worry too much about the type of biscuits and fruit. Feel free to mix and match depending on what is available.

- Lovely with a touch of crystallized or ground ginger.

The Dimbleby family in the Dordogne, 1976

Mum used to make this when we were kids. It is naughty, nostalgic and very nice. When we were taking the photographs for the book we left a whole cake on the side and in an hour noticed that it had gone. No one ever owned up.
Henry

From the top: Jossy' Casablanca Cakes;
Great Granny's Rock Buns;
Hannah's Welsh Cakes;
Mum's Chocolate & Fruit Biscuit Cake

JOSSY'S CASABLANCA CAKES

Perfect with ice cream (pictured on page 178).

(pictured on page 178)

Makes: 25–30
Preparation time: 15 minutes
Cooking time: 12 minutes

DF

50g **almonds**, with skins
1 **lemon**
1 large **egg**
100g **icing sugar**
½ teaspoon **baking powder**
100g **semolina**
extra **icing sugar** for dipping

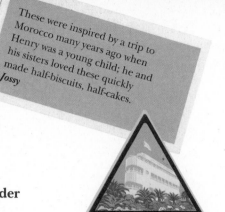

These were inspired by a trip to Morocco many years ago when Henry was a young child; he and his sisters loved these quickly made half-biscuits, half-cakes. *Jossy*

RECIPE TESTED BY JO & JAMES

1. Preheat the oven to 170°C/325°F/gas mark 3.

2. Put the almonds into a food processor and grind as finely as possible. Finely grate the lemon rind.

3. Whisk the egg with the icing sugar until very pale. Stir in the baking powder, semolina, ground almonds and lemon rind. Mix thoroughly.

4. Butter a large baking sheet and put some sieved icing sugar into a small bowl. Dampen your hands, take a piece of the mixture and form a ball the size of a large marble. Dip one side of the ball into the icing sugar and place it on the baking sheet, sugar side up.

5. Continue like this with the rest of the mixture, spacing the balls out 5cm apart as they spread quite a bit – you will probably have to cook them in two batches.

6. Bake the cakes in the centre of the oven for 10–12 minutes, until only very pale brown. Ease carefully off the baking sheet with a palette knife and cool on a rack.

HANNAH'S WELSH CAKES

Hannah and Xander put their faith (and some money) into Leon before we opened our first restaurant. They are both incurable enthusiasts and excellent cooks.

Makes: 12
Preparation time: 20 minutes
Cooking time: 10 minutes

V

230g **self-raising flour**
110g **butter**
85g **sugar**
55g **sultanas** or **currants**
1 **egg**

Hannah & her mum, 1978

1. Sieve the flour into a bowl, then rub in the butter until it is like fine breadcrumbs.

My mum's recipe from the Teifi Valley. When we visited Mount Vernon, George Washington's home in Virginia, there was a familiar smell of baking – it came from a group of actors who were cooking them over an open fire, and I recognized them as similar to the Welsh biscuits I had eaten as a child. *Hannah*

FRIENDS & FAMILY RECIPES

2. Add the sugar and dried fruit, and mix well. Beat the egg, add to the bowl and mix well until the mixture makes a ball.

3. Knead for a few minutes, then roll out on a floured board until 1cm thick. Cut into circular shapes.

4. Heat a little vegetable oil in a frying pan and fry the cakes on both sides for about 6–8 minutes in total. Be careful not to let them burn.

5. Leave to cool (see picture on page 178).

GREAT GRANNY'S ROCK BUNS

Makes: 12
Preparation time: 10 minutes
Cooking time: 15 minutes

180g **plain flour**
85g **butter**
85g **granulated sugar**
a pinch of **ground cinnamon**
1 teaspoon **baking powder**
85g **sultanas** or **currants**
1 small **egg**

Janet stepping out in Seaford, 1959

1. Preheat the oven to 180°C/350°F/gas mark 4.

2. Sieve the flour into a large clean bowl. Cut the butter into chunks and rub it in until it looks like breadcrumbs.

3. Add the sugar, cinnamon, baking powder and sultanas and mix thoroughly.

4. Whisk the egg and add it to the bowl, mixing it in with your hands. The mixture will seem dry but don't be alarmed – this is how rock buns are supposed to be.

5. Lightly flour a baking tray and arrange the mixture in 12 heaps, leaving plenty of space between for them to spread.

6. Bake for 15 minutes, or until golden brown (see picture on page 178).

The Lewis family in Beach Cottages, 1960

Our gran and her sister Betty used to make these from a recipe inherited from their grandmother, which makes us fifth-generation rock-bun makers. They should be firm when cool.
Hattie

SALLY DOLTON'S MUESLI BARS

Sally is a Leon regular who sent us this recipe for her muesli bars when we mentioned that we were writing a second cookbook. They are really, really good.

Makes: 16
Preparation time: 15 minutes
Cooking time: 20 minutes
♥ ✓ DF V

270g **dried fruit** (e.g. apricots, figs, dates, pears etc – a mixture or choose just one)
40g **nuts** (e.g. cashews)
80g **seeds** (e.g. pumpkin seeds, sunflower seeds)
1 teaspoon **ground cinnamon**
80ml **fruit juice** (e.g. apple or grape)
2 level tablespoons **honey**
60g **wholemeal flour**
120g rolled **oats**

1. Preheat the oven to 190°C/375°F/gas mark 5.

2. Put the dried fruit into a food processor and blitz until well chopped. Do the same with the nuts. Put the fruit, nuts, seeds and cinnamon into a bowl.

3. Warm the fruit juice and honey together in a pan large enough to eventually contain all the ingredients, until the honey is dissolved. Add the flour and oats, and stir in the fruit and nuts.

4. Smooth the mixture into a 25 x 30cm baking tray about 2.5cm deep. If the tray is not non-stick it is wise to line it with baking parchment.

5. Bake in the oven for 20 minutes – longer if you would like your bars more crunchy.

6. Allow to cool, then cut into rectangular bars. They will keep for 2 weeks in an airtight container.

TIPS
....

○ Try adding a handful of grated fresh ginger.

Nigel, Timmy and Sally strawberry-gorging in 1979

FRIENDS & FAMILY RECIPES

Glasgow Banana Bread (left) and Sally Dolton's Muesli Bars

GLASGOW BANANA BREAD

A wholesome fruity loaf (pictured on page 183).

Feeds: 4–6
Preparation time: 15 minutes
Cooking time: 30 minutes

v

2 **smallish eggs** (or 1 large)
125g **melted unsalted butter**
2–3 tablespoons **whole milk**, or more if needed
4 very ripe **bananas**
280g **spelt flour**
1 teaspoon **bicarbonate of soda**
2 tablespoons **wheatgerm** – optional
90g molasses or **muscovado sugar**
100g **cashew nuts**
90g **poppy seeds**
zest of 1 **lemon**
a pinch of **salt**

1. Heat the oven to 180°C/350°F/gas mark 4, and grease and line a 2lb loaf tin.

2. Whisk together the eggs, melted butter and milk. Mash up the bananas roughly and add to the mixture.

3. In a separate bowl sift together the spelt flour and bicarbonate of soda. Stir in the wheatgerm (if using), sugar, cashew nuts, poppy seeds, lemon zest and salt.

4. Gently fold the egg mixture into the dry ingredients – do not over-stir.

5. The mix should be a good dropping consistency – firm enough to stick to a spoon, but able to drop off if you turn it upside down. Add a little more flour or milk to get the correct consistency.

6. Put into the greased tin and bake for about 30 minutes, or until a knife comes out cleanly.

TIPS

o   If you would like the bread to have a Polish feel, add more poppy seeds.

o   You can also add dates, prunes or raisins, or some grated carrot, to diversify the banana flavour.

o   Serve it in slices, spread with butter.

Leon's opening day, July 2004 by Liza Dimbleby

My elder sister is an artist who lives in Glasgow but she pops into Leon whenever she is down south. On the day we opened in Carnaby Street she sat in the front of the restaurant sketching us for posterity.
Henry   LEON 2004

HENRY'S QUICK CHOCOLATE CAKE

This was the first cake I ever made, when I was about fifteen.

Feeds: 8
Preparation time: 10 minutes
Cooking time: 30 minutes
✓ WF GF V

8 medium **eggs**
400g **chocolate** (70 per cent cocoa solids)
150g **butter**
2 tablespoons **caster sugar**
350ml **crème fraîche**
zest of 1 **lemon**
pinch of **sea salt**

1. Preheat your oven to 180°C/350°F/gas mark 4, and butter 2 x 18cm circular cake tins. Separate the eggs, putting the yolks into a clean bowl and the whites into another. Whisk the egg yolks with a pinch of salt.

2. Melt the chocolate and butter in a large heatproof bowl placed over a pan of gently simmering water. Do not allow the chocolate to get too hot. Allow to cool for a couple of minutes, then fold the egg yolks into the chocolate and butter mix.

3. Whisk the egg whites to stiff peaks then whisk in the sugar. Fold them gently into the chocolate and egg yolk mixture. Pour the mixture into the cake tins, and cook in the oven for 15 minutes. Allow the cakes to cool on a rack (or in the fridge).

4. In a clean bowl mix together the crème fraîche and lemon zest, and use this to sandwich the cakes together.

5. To decorate the cake, cut a shape out of card, put it on top of the cake, and dust the top with icing sugar. Remove the card, leaving a nice shape in silhouette.

 TIPS

○ This cake is definitely grown-up – it's too strong for most young taste buds. You can add up to three times the quantity of sugar if you have a sweeter tooth.

 RECIPE TESTED BY PETRA

 RECIPE TESTED BY REBECCA

My mum used to make a similar cake to this and it has been adapted over the years. It is a super simple, dark, rich and low-sugar cake.
Henry

The first unveiling of the Leon Salted Caramel Banana Split (really)

PUDDINGS

PUDDING IS THE MOMENT
IN THE FEAST THAT
MAKES EVERYONE GO:
'WOW!'

CARAMELIZED PEAR FLAMBÉ *with quick real custard*

The custard method in this dish is another great tip from our friend Claire Cakes'. By using more cream and – critically – heating the sugar with the cream rather than adding it to the egg yolks, you eliminate the nervous stage of heating the custard over the stove and waiting for it to thicken, or, more often than not in my case, scramble. I never used to make custard but I make it all the time now. *Henry*

Feeds: 4
Preparation time: 10 minutes
Cooking time: 20 minutes

WF GF V

For the custard
5 **egg yolks**
1 **vanilla pod**
500ml **double cream**
100ml **milk**
180g **caster sugar**
sea salt

For the pears
1 large tablespoon **unsalted butter**
4 **pears**
2 tablespoons **brown sugar**
50ml **brandy** or **Cognac**, heated
   to boiling point

1. The eggs need to be at room temperature for this recipe.

2. Halve the vanilla pod lengthways and put it in a pan with the cream, milk and caster sugar. Bring to the boil, stirring to make sure the sugar dissolves. Take the pan off the heat and allow it to sit for 5 minutes.

3. Meanwhile, put the egg yolks into a blender and blend for 2 minutes, or until they go creamy. Add a small pinch of salt.

4. Bring the cream back to the boil and pour it slowly on to the eggs, blending as you go. Assuming that the cream is good and hot and the eggs not too cold, the result should be great not-too-thick custard. (If you want to make it thicker you can pour it into a pan and heat it gently on the hob, but you shouldn't need to.)

5. Peel, core and halve the pears. Put a wide frying pan on a high heat. Add the butter, then the pears, and toss until well coated. Sprinkle on the brown sugar. Toss for another 4 minutes, until tinged with brown, well coated with the caramel and tender.

6. Get everyone's attention, stand back, and pour in the brandy or Cognac – it should flame. When the flames have gone out, serve with the custard.

FRIENDS & FAMILY
RECIPES

LEON SALTED CARAMEL BANANA SPLIT

Feeds: 6
Preparation time: 10 minutes
Cooking time: 10 minutes
WF GF V

100g organic **flaked almonds**
2 tablespoons organic **icing sugar**
6 Fairtrade **bananas**
500ml organic **double cream**
100g Fairtrade **caster sugar**
500ml organic **vanilla ice cream**
250ml organic **strawberry ice cream**
25g organic **dark chocolate**
sea salt

1. Heat the almonds in a non-stick frying pan with the icing sugar until they turn golden and the sugar has caramelized. Put into a bowl and set aside.

2. Halve the bananas lengthways and lay two halves on each plate.

3. Whisk 350ml of the cream until thick. Put into a piping bag (a squirty cream thing available online, saves time here).

4. Heat the caster sugar in a pan until it has melted and caramelized, but is not too dark. Add the remaining 150ml of cream and stir well. It will froth right up. Heat through to make sure all the sugar has melted into the cream, stirring occasionally. Add a good pinch of salt.

5. Put 2 scoops of vanilla and one of strawberry ice cream on to each split banana.

6. Drizzle the ice cream with the caramel. Pipe on the cream, sprinkle with the almonds, grate over some chocolate and serve.

  TIPS

○ For the truly classic split, top each scoop of ice cream with a glacé cherry.

○ In the restaurants we use a runny blackcurrant compote alongside the caramel as a second sauce.

LONDON W1F 7JE
LEON.
35-36 Gt. MARLBOROUGH St.
Fair Trade & Organic
NOME DEL PASSEGGERO
BAGAGLIAIO

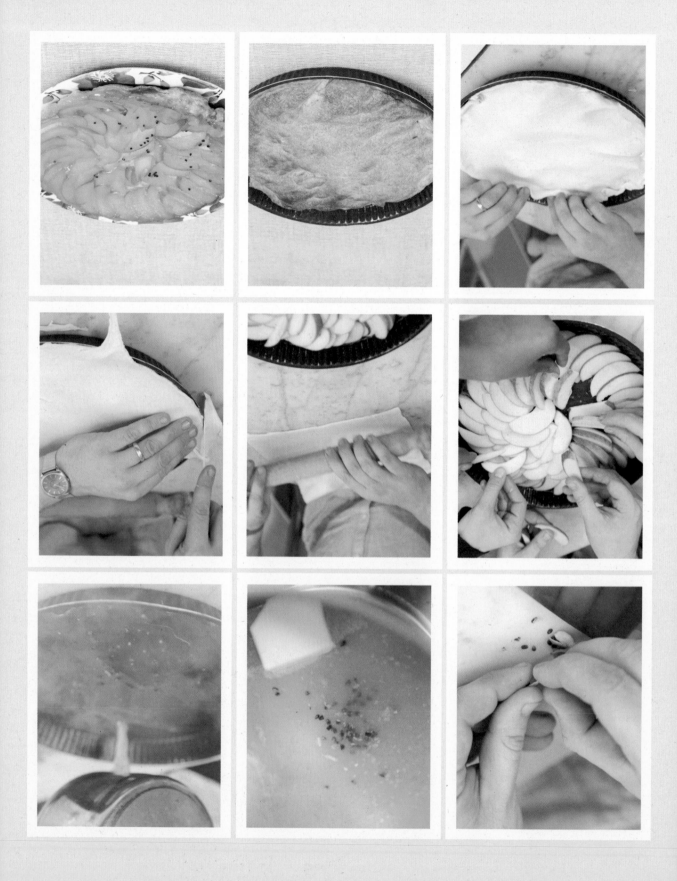

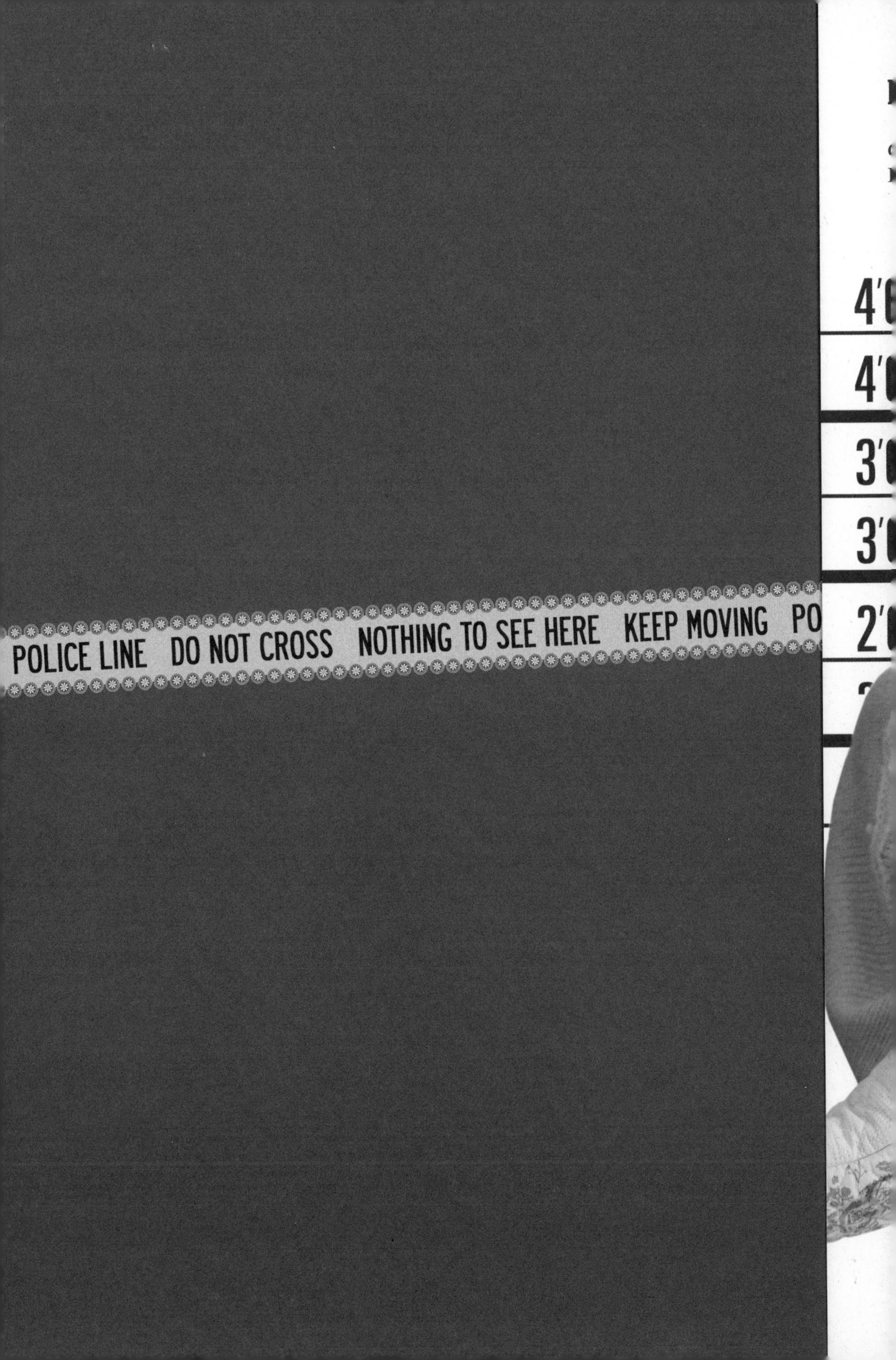

POLICE LINE   DO NOT CROSS   NOTHING TO SEE HERE   KEEP MOVING   PO

4'6

4'0

3'0

3'0

2'0

RESSING UP *shop-bought ice cream*

One of the simplest ways to create a sensational pudding is to buy vanilla ice cream and dress it up. Here are some of our usual suspects:

HAZELNUT CRACKNELL

Sweet and crunchy. Melt 200g sugar in a non pan. Toss in 80g hazelnuts and pour onto an greaseproof sheet. When it is cold, wrap the w thing in a tea towel and give it a satisfying sma with a rolling pin.

CARAMELIZED BISCUITS

Sweet and crispy. Crush 5 digestive biscuits and heat in a non-stick pan with 2 tablespoons caster sugar until the sugar has melted. Stir often and watch it carefully to make sure it doesn't burn.

SPICED RED WINE SYRUP

A little bit of posh. Boil up 500ml red wine with 100g fructose, 1 cinnamon stick, 4 cardamom pods and 2 star anise. Reduce to a syrup.

MARS BAR SAUCE

The devil may claim
Simply melt 3 Mars b
tell a soul. Stir thoro
well. It should take a

UPSIDE-DOWN APPLE & CARDAMOM TART

The flavour of the cardamom transforms this simple apple tart.

Feeds: 4
Preparation time: 10 minutes
Cooking time: 30 minutes

3 cardamom pods
juice of 1 orange
4 tablespoons soft brown sugar
40g butter
4 apples (about 650g)
200g puff pastry

1. Preheat the oven to 180°C/350°F/gas mark 4.

2. Crush the cardamom pods and keep the little seeds. In a saucepan heat the orange juice, sugar, butter and cardamom seeds until thick and bubbly. Pour the syrup into a 25cm flan tin (obviously it cannot be one with a push-out bottom or it will seep though and go everywhere).

3. Quarter the apples and cut out the cores. Cut each quarter into thin slices and arrange symmetrically on top of the syrup in the flan tin.

4. Roll out your pastry and lay it over the top of the tin. Cut off the excess around the edges. Sprinkle a little more sugar on top if you like.

5. Place the tin in the oven for 30 minutes, or until the pastry has risen and is golden. Put a serving plate on top, hold it tightly and flip the whole thing over. Tap the bottom of the tin to ensure that all the apple slices are on the plate, and remove it. A magically neat and tidy tart will appear.

TIPS

o Serve with cream or Quick Real Custard (see page 190).

o This is one of those versatile recipes. You can use almost any fruit – pears, plums, apricots, nectarines, peaches and oranges all work well. You can also play with the syrup: try a red wine syrup with star anise and plums. White wine, vanilla and nectarine make a subtle combination; with oranges, try using shortcrust pastry and a really treacly syrup made with a little molasses as well as sugar.

o When using soft fruit in this tart it is better if the fruit is slightly under-ripe.

RECIPE TESTED BY. BAMBI
RECIPE TESTED BY. PETRA
RECIPE TESTED BY. KATE

DO NOT CROSS   NOTHING TO SEE HERE   KEEP MOVING   POLICE LINE   DO NOT CROSS

...hey make a syrup. Toss in 300g mixed berries ... the juices are starting to thicken. (You can ...nom – for extra flavour if you like.)

4'6"
4'0"
3'6"
3'0"
2'6"
2'0"
1'6"
1'0"

Quick Berry Compote

If you want to make your own home-made ice cream, see the recipes on pages 273–4.

, but this is heaven on earth.
s in 150ml double cream and don't
hly to ensure they have blended
ut 10 minutes.

QUICK BERRY COMPOTE

Heat 4 tablespoons water and 4 tablespoons sugar in a pan until
and cook for a couple of minutes, until the fruit has softened an
add some sweet spice – e.g. vanilla, star anise, cinnamon or card

RUM & RAISIN

One for the grown-ups.
Heat 250ml rum with
2 tablespoons of raisins
or sultanas and
2 tablespoons caster
sugar. Flame off the
alcohol and allow the
flame to burn for a few
minutes. Reduce to a
syrupy consistency,
which should take
about 15 minutes.

Mars Bar
sauce

Rum
&
Raisin

PIERRE'S PAIN PERDU

Literally 'lost bread', this is a great French way to use up stale bread, and is even better made with brioche.

Feeds: 4
Preparation time: 5 minutes
Cooking time: 12 minutes

(V)

1 (stale) **baguette**
150ml **milk**
25g **butter**, plus a little extra
2–3 heaped tablespoons **light brown sugar**

1. Cut the bread into 3cm-thick diagonal slices. Put the slices into a dish where they will all fit tightly, then pour over the milk and leave for 10 minutes so that they absorb all the milk.

2. Gently heat the butter in a large frying pan. When it starts to foam, sprinkle each piece of bread on one side with half the sugar and put the slices into the frying pan, sugar side down to caramelize.

3. After about 3–4 minutes, sprinkle over the remaining sugar then turn over the slices to caramelize the other side.

4. The pain perdu should become nicely caramelized. When it's ready, add another small knob of butter to the pan just before serving.

TIPS

o Add chopped dried fruit such as apricots and sultanas to the bread when you sprinkle over the sugar.

o You can also flambé this pudding with Calvados or brandy.

o Great with crème fraîche and fruit compote, or vanilla ice cream.

My friend Pierre loves pudding. At a dinner I cooked for him the other day he was so disappointed that there wasn't any pudding that he got up and cooked this himself. It was mighty fine. *Henry*

FRIENDS & FAMILY RECIPES

Pierre

Amaretti & Raspberry
Pud is a real chalet
girl special – always
a regular dish when
I was a chalet girl in
Val d'Isère. The
wonderful John
Yates Smith always
thought this was fab!
So easy yet very
impressive! *Apple*

FRIENDS & FAMILY
RECIPES

MIXED FRUIT *with Greek yoghurt & brown molasses sugar*

A straightforward pudding that can be made a few hours in advance. People always assume that it involves some complicated brûlée action, which is pleasing.

Feeds: 4
Preparation time: 10 minutes
Cooking time: 0 minutes
WF GF V

1 large ripe **mango**
1 **kiwi fruit**
100g **blueberries** or **blackberries**
100g **strawberries**
1 **passion fruit**
500g tub of **Greek yoghurt**
3–4 heaped tablespoons **dark brown molasses sugar**

1. Peel and chop the mango and kiwi into cubes and place in a large mixing bowl.

2. Add the berries and the passion fruit seeds and mix well.

3. Chose an attractive serving bowl, or individual bowls if you want, and spoon in the chopped fruit.

4. Top generously with the Greek yoghurt, so that it covers all the fruit in a thick layer.

5. Scatter over the molasses sugar – it will start to soak into the yoghurt, but you will notice that some remains in clumps and forms delicious toffee-like blobs.

TIPS

○ Add more sugar if you like it swimming in the melted molasses.

○ If you are making this in advance, you can either add the sugar just before serving, or add it earlier, let it soak into the yoghurt and add extra at the last minute.

○ Use any combination of fruit. Berries and stoned fruits work the best.

APPLE'S BREATHTAKINGLY QUICK CHOCOLATE POTS

Makes: 6 little pots
Preparation time: 5 minutes, plus 2 hours in the fridge
Cooking time: 0 hours
WF GF V

240ml **double cream**
70g **caster sugar**
200g **chocolate**
1 teaspoon **vanilla essence**
2 **egg yolks**

1. Heat the cream and sugar in a pan and bring to the boil. Stir well to dissolve the sugar.

2. Chop the chocolate into small chunks and put into a food processor with the vanilla essence and egg yolks.

3. When the cream is simmering, start the processor and pour it in. When smooth, pour the mixture into small coffee cups or ramekins and refrigerate for at least 2 hours.

APPLE'S AMARETTI & RASPBERRY PUD

This takes no time at all and, like Apple, looks spectacular.

Feeds: 4
Preparation time: 10 minutes
Cooking time: 0 minutes v

300ml **double cream**
300ml **crème fraîche**
1 teaspoon **vanilla essence**
100g **amaretti biscuits**
200g **raspberries**

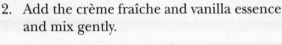

1. Whisk the cream until thick but still pourable, like a custard.

2. Add the crème fraîche and vanilla essence and mix gently.

3. Crush the amaretti biscuits and set aside a few for the top of the dish. Layer most of the raspberries with the amaretti and cream in glasses or a glass dish, then repeat the layers.

4. Finish with the rest of the raspberries and sprinkle with the reserved amaretti.

TIPS

○ Make this the night before, or at least 4 hours before your guests arrive.

CLAIRE'S RHUBARB & AMARETTI TART

This tart looks crazy when you put it into the oven with its beehive of rhubarb stacked on top – but it comes out a simple and impressive finale to a good Sunday lunch.

Feeds: 6
Preparation time: 5 minutes
Cooking time: 30–35 minutes
*

1 x 375g ready-made roll of **puff pastry**, fresh or frozen
80g **amaretti** biscuits
500g **rhubarb**
100g **sugar**

1. Heat the oven to 200°C/400°F/gas mark 6.

2. Unroll the pastry and place it on a well-greased baking sheet that has been lined with greaseproof paper. Fold over the sides to make an edge and press down with a fork. Crumble the amaretti biscuits and scatter over the bottom of the tart.

3. Cut the rhubarb stems in half, then slice into long thin strips and put into a bowl.

4. When you are ready to cook the tart, toss the rhubarb in the sugar and immediately stack it on top of the pastry and put it into the oven. If you wait it will start to produce a lot of liquid.

5. Cook for 35–40 minutes, until the pastry is a light golden colour.

TIPS

o If you are using frozen pastry, allow time for it to defrost. If it's not already rolled, roll it out into a rectangle about 35 x 25cm.

o Serve with cream or Quick Real Custard (see page 190).

o Brush the pastry with beaten egg yolk before cooking for a glazed finish.

FRIENDS & FAMILY
RECIPES

5   6   7   8

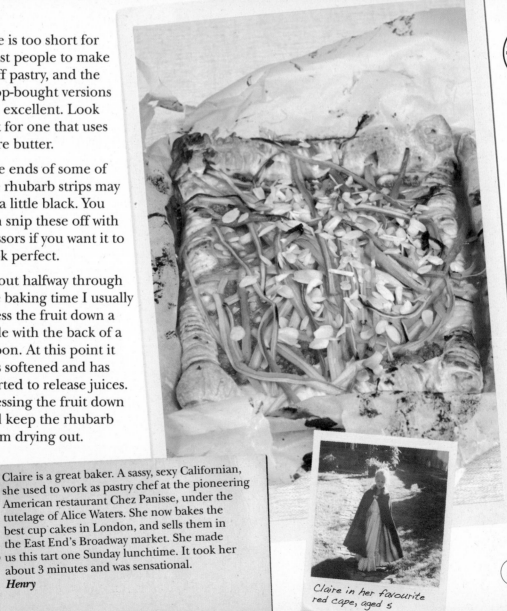

- Life is too short for most people to make puff pastry, and the shop-bought versions are excellent. Look out for one that uses pure butter.

- The ends of some of the rhubarb strips may go a little black. You can snip these off with scissors if you want it to look perfect.

- About halfway through the baking time I usually press the fruit down a little with the back of a spoon. At this point it has softened and has started to release juices. Pressing the fruit down will keep the rhubarb from drying out.

Claire is a great baker. A sassy, sexy Californian, she used to work as pastry chef at the pioneering American restaurant Chez Panisse, under the tutelage of Alice Waters. She now bakes the best cup cakes in London, and sells them in the East End's Broadway market. She made us this tart one Sunday lunchtime. It took her about 3 minutes and was sensational.
Henry

Claire in her favourite red cape, aged 5

RECIPE TESTED BY LILLIE & PETRA

201

Illustration by
Flora McEvedy

FOOD

People get too worked up about throwing parties. All you need is lovely people, decent food, music and booze. And if any of the former isn't quite spot on, judicious application of the latter will plaster over the cracks. These easy snacks should make your party go with a...

BANG!

70s Party

A party spread made up from the guilty secrets of friends and family.

FEEDS: 8

PREPARATION TIME: 10 MINUTES
COOKING TIME: 0 MINUTES

Laura with her siblings and grandparents, 1986

Laura's smokin' mackerel dip with melba toast

♥ ✓

Serve with melba toast, platform shoes and flares.

Laura and her sister 'Party Polly' have been helping us organize parties and events for Leon since we opened.

4 fillets **smoked mackerel** – about 350g
1 **fresh red chilli**
zest and juice of ½ a **lime**
pinch of **ground cumin**
2 tablespoons **horseradish cream**
200g **cream cheese**
10 slices of **sliced white bread**
sea salt and **freshly ground black pepper**

1. Skin the mackerel, break it up into small bits and put it into a bowl.
2. Deseed the chilli, chop it finely and add it to the mackerel.
3. Add the lime zest and juice, cumin, horseradish and cream cheese.
4. Toast the bread in a toaster and cut off the crusts. Split the bread horizontally through the middle and toast the untoasted side of each slice under the grill.
5. Serve with the mackerel dip and crunchy carrot sticks.

RECIPE TESTED BY GEORGIE

Everything can be made in advance except for the puff pastry swirls, which are best eaten straight from the oven.

Xander's puff pastry swirls

Party savouries recipe

2

FEEDS: 8
PREPARATION TIME: 20 MINUTES
COOKING TIME: 25 MINUTES

Xander has been a long-standing Leon lover. He is also a great host. If you are lucky enough to be invited to his for dinner you will probably get these as a canapé.

90g pitted **black olives**
50g **capers**
25g **anchovies** (½ a small tin)
1 x 500g packet of frozen **puff pastry**
2 large pinches of **dried chilli flakes**
10 **sun-dried tomatoes**
1 **egg**, beaten
freshly ground black pepper

1. Preheat the oven to 220°C/425°F/gas mark 7.
2. Drain the olives, capers and anchovies and chop them together roughly.
3. Roll out your puff pastry to a thickness of a few millimetres in a long rectangle. With the long side of the rectangle facing you, spread the olive mixture evenly on to the pastry, leaving a 3cm border round the edge. Season with pepper.
4. Sprinkle the chilli flakes over the mixture. Slice the sun-dried tomatoes and sprinkle those over too. Gently roll up the pastry into a log. Seal the edge by dampening it with water. Refrigerate for 30 minutes.
5. Using a sharp knife and a sawing motion, cut off rounds 1cm thick and place them on a well greased baking tray, leaving plenty of room between each one for them to spread.
6. Brush the rounds with beaten egg and bake for 20 minutes. They may need a further 5 minutes to brown up the centres.

TIPS You can make the log in advance and freeze it until required and then just slice and cook from frozen.

RECIPE TESTED BY PETRA

Xander and his family, Ireland, 1979

Jossy's Vodka, chilli cherry tomatoes

550g **cherry tomatoes**
150ml **sherry**
350ml **vodka**
1 teaspoon **cayenne pepper**
sea salt and **freshly ground black pepper**

1. Wash the cherry tomatoes and prick all over with a toothpick.
2. Mix the sherry, vodka and cayenne in a jar with a lid and add salt and pepper.
3. Drop the cherry tomatoes into the jar and let them sink into the liquid. Seal. This recipe should make enough to fill 2 x 450g jars. Leave in a cool place for 3 days.
4. Open the jar and serve.

TIPS Try not to squash them, but nestle them in so they are all snug and no space is wasted.

FEEDS: A SMALL PARTY
PREPARATION TIME: 24–36 HOURS
COOKING TIME: 0 MINUTES
♥ ✓ WF DF GF Ve

A chef I met a long time ago gave me this recipe. I did it for a drinks party and people got VERY intoxicated but loved them.
Jossy

FEEDS: 4
PREPARATION TIME: 5 MINUTES
COOKING TIME: 15 MINUTES

Henry's sweet and sour prawns

8 **raw prawns**
1 small **fresh red chilli**
a 2.5cm piece of **fresh ginger**
8 teaspoons **rice vinegar**
6 teaspoons **honey**
1 teaspoon **vegetable oil**
a pinch of **sea salt**

1. Peel the prawns but leave the tails on. Deseed the chilli and chop finely. Finely chop the ginger. Put the chilli and ginger into a pan over a low heat with the vinegar and honey, and simmer until the sauce has reduced to a coating consistency.
2. Fry the prawns in the vegetable oil for about a minute and a half on each side (or cook them on a griddle). Season well and drop into the sauce. Serve.

Henry on his 5th birthday, 1975

PREPARATION TIME: 20 MINUTES
COOKING TIME: 15 MINUTES (APPROX)
FEEDS 8–10

Jossy's quick cheese straws

Party savouries recipe
5

Although these are made with wholemeal flour, they are deliciously light.

150g **mature Cheddar** or other strong cheese
2 teaspoons **paprika**
100g **plain wholemeal flour**
2 teaspoons **baking powder**
100g **unsalted butter**
2 **egg yolks**

1. Preheat the oven to 220°C/425°F/gas mark 7.
2. Grate the cheese and put into a mixing bowl. Mix the paprika into the flour and then into the cheese. Cut the butter into small pieces and rub into the flour and cheese with your fingertips. Add the baking powder.
3. Add the egg yolks and mix to a stiff dough with a wooden spoon.
4. Using floured hands, gather the dough into a ball and, on a floured board, press out with the palms of your hands until about 1cm thick.
5. Cut into straws – they can be varying lengths, but should be about 2cm wide – and place on a large ungreased baking sheet.
6. Bake the straws at the top of the oven for 8–12 minutes, until golden brown.

Jossy, 1976

TIPS

You can vary the flavour of these by substituting mild curry powder, caraway seeds or other spices for the paprika. The straws are irresistible while still slightly warm, but any that survive can be kept for several days in an airtight container.

Our friend Kamal lives in Beirut and knows how to throw a party. This menu is inspired by an evening we spent in Mounir – a massive restaurant on the hillside that overlooks the city – drinking arak and eating till we popped.

You can make everything except the halloumi in advance.

This feast will serve 8 well. Great with ice cold arak (arak is never drunk from the fridge… it must be made cold with ice cubes).

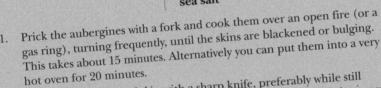

KAMAL'S AUBERGINE PURÉE

Kamal is very particular about his moutabal, especially that it should not contain garlic. This is the best we have ever tasted. (If you make it with yoghurt instead of tahini it becomes babaganoush – in the Syrian way.)

Feeds: 4 as part of a mezze
Preparation time: 20 minutes
Cooking time: 0 minutes

1kg large **aubergines**
125ml **tahini**
juice of 3 **lemons**
2 tablespoons **olive oil**
sea salt

RECIPE TESTED BY JACKIE

1. Prick the aubergines with a fork and cook them over an open fire (or a gas ring), turning frequently, until the skins are blackened or bulging. This takes about 15 minutes. Alternatively you can put them into a very hot oven for 20 minutes.
2. Peel off the blackened skin with a sharp knife, preferably while still warm, and either mash the inside with a fork or whizz in a food processor.
3. Add the tahini and lemon juice and season with salt.
4. Serve with a drizzle of olive oil.

GRILLED HALLOUMI

Squeaky cheese. We love it, and it has been a fixture on the Leon dinner menu since we opened.

Simply grill or griddle sliced halloumi on a low heat until turning a crispy brown (which should take 3 to 4 minutes), and serve with a squeeze of lemon.

You can add a mint, parsley and a toasted seed topper to liven it up if you like.

TURKISH ALMOND DIP

You can cut any vegetables you like into sticks or pieces to eat with this nutty dip.

25g good **white bread**, crusts removed
50g **unsalted almonds**, in their skins
1 large clove of **garlic**
2 tablespoons **lemon juice**
75ml **extra virgin olive oil**
50ml **sunflower oil**
2 heaped tablespoons **full-fat natural yoghurt**
a little **milk**
sea salt and **freshly ground black pepper**

1. Dip the bread into a bowl of water and squeeze dry.
2. Put the almonds into a food processor and whizz until they are as fine as possible.
3. Crush or grate the garlic and add to the processor, along with the soaked bread, lemon juice, both the oils and the yoghurt.
4. Whizz until smooth, adding a little milk if it seems too thick, and season to taste.
5. Spoon into a serving bowl and refrigerate for 30 minutes or more. Before serving with the prepared vegetables, trickle over a spoonful of olive oil.

RECIPE TESTED BY GEORGIE

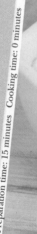

Preparation time: 15 minutes Cooking time: 0 minutes

eparation time: 5 minutes Cooking time: 5 minutes

HUMMUS TOPPER

Use shop-bought hummus or the recipe from the first Leon cookbook and jazz it up with this meaty topper.

½ a **red pepper**
1 tablespoon **olive oil**
1 tablespoon **cumin seeds**
150g **minced lamb**
a squeeze of **lemon juice**
sea salt and **freshly ground black pepper**

1. Finely dice the red pepper.
2. In a frying pan heat the olive oil, add the pepper and cook for a minute.
3. Add the cumin seeds and the minced lamb and season with salt and pepper.
4. Frazzle on a high heat until the meat is crispy and cooked through.
5. Squeeze over some lemon juice, then scatter the lamb mix over your hummus.

RECIPE TESTED BY TARQUIN

TZATSIKI

1 **cucumber**
½ a clove of **garlic**
a handful of **fresh mint**
250ml **natural yoghurt**
a squeeze of **lemon juice**
sea salt and **freshly ground black pepper**

1. Halve the cucumber lengthwise and scrape out the seeds, then grate. Scatter with salt and leave for a few minutes, then squeeze out well and put into a large bowl.
2. Finely chop the garlic and mint. Add to the yoghurt along with the cucumber, and stir well.
3. Season with salt and pepper, and add lemon juice to taste.

RECIPE TESTED BY LUCY

Parties have always been a big part of Leon life. The best kind are the ones where it gets to one in the morning and your granny is still on the dance floor and the kids are bouncing around her knees. No one does this like the Spanish. Any nation that starts going out for dinner at 10 p.m. has partying in its blood.

Everything can be made in advance, with the exception of the papas con chorizo. Serve it all with some chunks of good bread and olive oil for dipping.

This spread will serve 8 comfortably.

Papas con chorizo

A twist on the classic tapas dish, using sweet potatoes in place of potatoes..

Preparation time: 5 minutes
Cooking time: 35–40 minutes
✓ WF DF GF

6 raw **chorizo sausages**
3 large **sweet potatoes**
1 tablespoon **olive oil**
1 tablespoon **fennel seeds**
1 tablespoon **chilli flakes**
(we like the less hot oily ones)
sea salt and **freshly ground black pepper**

1. Preheat the oven to 180°C/350°F/gas mark 4. Cut the chorizo into horizontal slices.
2. Peel the sweet potatoes and cut into 2cm cubes. Put into a large baking tray. Add the olive oil, fennel seeds, chilli flakes and seasoning, and mix thoroughly with your hands.
3. Put into the oven. After 20 minutes add the chorizo to the tray and cook for a further 15 minutes.

Rosemary Toasted Almonds

This is our friend Claire's recipe and is a fixture on the Leon dinner menu.

Preparation time: 2 minutes
Cooking time: 10 minutes
♥ ✓ WF DF GF V

500g **whole almonds**, with skins
6 sprigs of **fresh rosemary**
50ml **extra virgin olive oil**
sea salt

1. Preheat the oven to 170°C/325°F/gas mark 3.
2. Spread the almonds out evenly on a baking sheet (no more than 3 layers deep). Add 4 of the rosemary sprigs. Remove the leaves from the remaining sprigs and set aside.
3. Toast in the oven for about 7 minutes, or until just starting to go brown.
4. While still hot, toss with the olive oil and salt. Remove and discard the rosemary sprigs and add the reserved leaves. Return to the oven for 3 more minutes, until the almonds are fully toasted. Do not over-toast, or they will go bitter.

Claire making an 'experiment' cake, aged 5

Spanish Party

Manchego & Quince Jelly

This Spanish cheese is now available in good supermarkets and at many of the food markets that are popping up around the country. It has a supernatural affinity with quinces and ice-cold beer. You can serve it with shop-bought membrillo (a kind of thick paste made from quinces) or with Petra's Quince Jelly on page 261.

Boquerones (Pickled Anchovies)

You can now buy these from most supermarkets. It is important to get the pickled ones – not the salted ones, or the ones in tins. Simply drizzle them with good olive oil and sprinkle with roughly chopped parsley. Serve with toothpicks to skewer them into the mouth.

SLOW
FAST
FOOD

This section is about dishes that you can cook in advance and whip out at speed when you want them.

While these recipes may take a little longer to cook, we have done our best to ensure that they remain simple. Many of them are actually very quick to prepare, but need longer bubbling on the heat. Once cooked, they are brilliant reheated: ideal to pop into the oven while you put your feet up with a glass of wine.

THE SCIENCE BIT

> In short: either cook your meat hot and fast or long and gentle.
> Anything between is liable to end in toughness.

The next two sections – Slow Cooks and Pot Roasts – deal with food that needs to cook slowly so that the flavours mix, mellow and mature. While there are some vegetarian recipes here, this is principally a style of cooking that is used for meat, which is where the science comes in.

Meat is made up of juicy muscle cells and connecting fibres. The connecting fibres are made principally of collagen, which is tough. To make your meat tender and delicious, you have three options:

Option 1

Buy more expensive cuts of meat (which tend not to have much connecting fibre) and cook them quickly. The juicy muscle cells stay intact and retain their moisture. The result is a succulent morsel – think good steak, pink lamb chops or grilled chicken breast.

If you cook the meat for a little too long, however, the muscle cells start to break and lose their moisture and the meat gets tough. This happens at different temperatures for different meats. Using a meat thermometer, with the probe inside the thickest part of the cut, can ensure that you get it right every time.

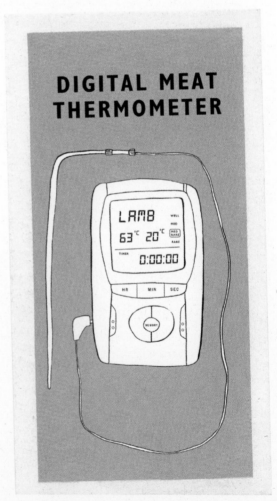

DIGITAL MEAT THERMOMETER

INTERNAL TEMPERATURES FOR PERFECTLY COOKED
MEAT

BEEF
Very rare . . . . .54°C
Rare . . . . .60°C
Medium rare . . . . .63°C
Medium
(still a little pink) . . . . .68°C

LAMB
Rare . . . . .60°C
Medium . . . . .63°C

CHICKEN (and other poultry)
Succulent . . . . .74°C

PORK
Succulent . . . . .66°C

Option 2

Take a cheaper cut of meat, with more tough connecting tissue, and cook it for longer. This is the method most often used in the following pages. As they pass the temperatures in the table above, the muscle cells burst, releasing their moisture (which initially makes the meat go tough). Prolonged cooking in liquid, however, leads to the breaking down of the collagen and the reabsorption of the liquid, creating the familiar soft flavours and textures of braised meat.

The only way you can go wrong here is to get stuck between Option 1 and Option 2 – muscle cells burst but collagen is still intact – in which case your meat will be tough. Don't worry: just pop it back into the oven. It will only get better. (And you can add a little water, wine or stock if the dish as a whole is drying out.)

Option 3

The invention of accurate meat thermometers and electric ovens that can hold temperatures consistently has led in recent years to a third way.

By happy scientific coincidence, collagen starts to break down at around 50°C but cell walls only start to burst (and lose their fluid) at around 60°C. Therefore if you take the temperature of your meat up incredibly slowly and leave it at around 55°C for 10 hours or more, the collagen will dissolve while the cell walls stay intact. This means the final result will be unbelievably tender but also pink and juicy.

This is new-style slow cooking and has become fashionable in fancy restaurants, as the results can be mind-blowing. It is tricky to do, but deeply satisfying when you get it right. All you need is an oven that will hold an accurate – and sufficiently low – temperature, plus a meat thermometer. The only drawback of this method is that it doesn't make any juice for gravy.

HENRY'S 18-HOUR BEEF

A great dish to make when you want to go out on Saturday night, read the papers on Sunday morning and still have 15 people round for Sunday lunch.

Saturday night 8 p.m. (if you do it a couple of hours earlier that would be fine too):

1. Before you go out, set your oven to 60°C. Check that it is stable at this temperature by putting the meat probe in the oven and checking it after 10 minutes. If you can't get your oven to be stable at 60°C, you can't cook beef like this. Sorry. (With my oven, I have to tap the temperature gauge around a bit to get it just right. A digital temperature setting would make things easier.)

2. Smear the outside of a good-sized cut of beef (I like rib on the bone) with copious coarse-ground black pepper and Dijon or wholegrain mustard. Heat a roasting tray on the hob until very hot, add some oil and sear the beef so it goes a crisp, golden brown on all sides – the way you want it to look when you serve it up.

3. Put the probe thermometer into the centre of the beef and put it, still in the roasting tray, into the 60°C oven.

4. Go out.

Saturday before you go to bed:

1. Check the thermometer (no need to open the oven) – if it is above 50°C already it probably means your oven is too high. Take the probe out of the beef and leave it on the rack in the oven so that you can check the oven temperature. Once you are confident that the oven is at 60°C, put the probe back in and go to bed.

Sunday morning:

1. Turn the oven up to 65°C.

2. While you are reading the papers, check every half hour or so as the temperature rises. Very rare is 55°C. Medium 60°C. I think it is perfect at 58°C. The temperatures rise very slowly, so it is easy to hit the required one. Once the meat is done – this should be around 1 p.m. – set the oven to the same temperature

(i.e. if you want it very rare, set it to 55°C). The meat will just sit at that temperature now, getting more and more tender. You can leave it as long as necessary without worrying (in fact you could eat it for dinner if you wanted – it will only get more tender).

Sunday 2 p.m. (or 3 p.m. or 4 p.m. or 5 p.m. or whenever):

1. Pull out the beef. No need to rest it. Just carve it when you are ready.

GRAVY

As the beef doesn't produce any juice when you cook it this way, you will have to make gravy from a previously made stock. Or alternatively, serve it as I normally do, with a béarnaise and/or some creamy horseradish. (For fresh horseradish sauce, grate the root and mix it with lightly whipped cream or natural yoghurt, vinegar, English mustard, salt and pepper.)

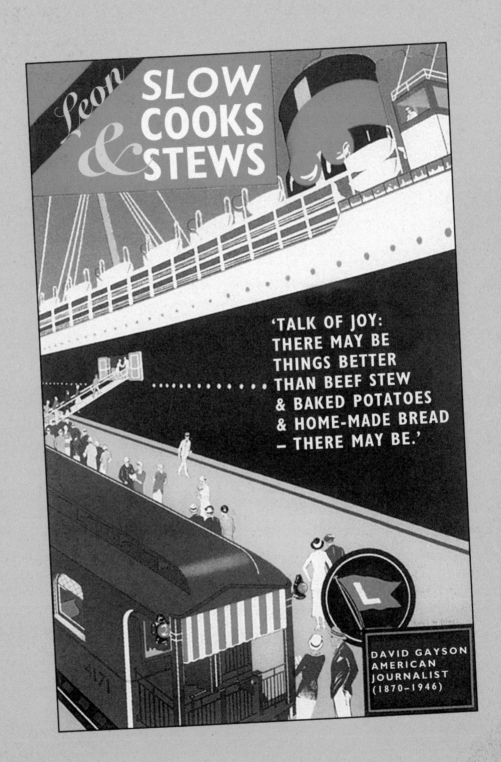

LEON CHILLI CON CARNE

A classic chilli, now a fixture on the Leon menu – a great dish to prepare in advance and freeze.

Feeds: 6–8
Preparation time: 10 minutes
Cooking time: 2 hours
✓ WF DF GF

3 **carrots**
2 **onions**
4 cloves of **garlic**
2 sticks of **celery**
3 tablespoons **olive oil**
1kg **minced beef**
3 **bay leaves**
2 teaspoons **ground cumin**
1 teaspoons **oregano**
6 tablespoons **tomato purée**
3 x 400g tins **chopped tomatoes**
2 teaspoons **smoked sweet paprika**
3 teaspoons **cayenne pepper**
100ml **malt vinegar**
2 x 400g tins **kidney beans**, drained
sea salt and **freshly ground black pepper**

1. Peel and quarter the carrots and onions and put in a food processor. Peel the garlic and add it along with the celery, then blitz until they are all very finely chopped.

2. Heat the oil in a large saucepan and add the blitzed vegetables. Fry over a gentle heat until the vegetables have softened.

3. Add the minced beef and cook for 10 minutes, or until it is brown all over. Then add the rest of the ingredients and stir well. Cook for 2 hours on the hob, uncovered, stirring now and then. Add a little water if necessary to prevent it from drying out.

Henry and Mima

FRIENDS & FAMILY RECIPES

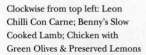

Clockwise from top left: Leon Chilli Con Carne; Benny's Slow Cooked Lamb; Chicken with Green Olives & Preserved Lemons

We'd been working on a classic chilli dish for a while when my wife Mima by coincidence cooked me this one at home. Quest ended. It went straight on the menu.
Henry

BENNY'S SLOW-COOKED LAMB
with kohlrabi & Indian spices

Kohlrabi is becoming increasingly available, and is great for slow-cooked dishes because it keeps its shape (pictured on page 218).

Feeds: 4
Preparation time: 20 minutes
Cooking time: 4 hours
✓ WF GF

800g **shoulder of lamb**
500g **onions**
1.5kg **kohlrabi** (about 3, medium size)
a 3cm piece of **fresh ginger**
4 tablespoons **rapeseed oil**
200ml **natural yoghurt**
2 tablespoons **medium curry powder**
1 teaspoon **garam masala**
a handful of toasted flaked **almonds**
sea salt and **freshly ground black pepper**

1. Preheat the oven to 150°C/300°F/gas mark 2. Cut the lamb into 5cm cubes. Cut the onions into thin rings. Peel and dice the kohlrabi. Finely chop the ginger.

2. Heat the oil in a heavy-based casserole pan over a medium heat. Add the onions and a sprinkling of salt and cook for 15 minutes, or until caramelized and brown.

3. Add the lamb and ginger. Season and stir. Turn down to a low heat, add the yoghurt and bring to the boil.

4. Add the curry powder and stir for a minute or so. Pour in about 1 litre of water, or enough to cover the lamb comfortably, then add the kohlrabi and bring to a gentle simmer.

5. Cover with a lid, place in the oven and cook for 3 hours, stirring every hour or so.

6. Stir in the garam masala and check the seasoning, then sprinkle the toasted almonds over the curry and serve.

TIPS

○ Serve with basmati rice (see recipe on page 86).

Little Benny, 1983

FRIENDS & FAMILY RECIPES

CHICKEN WITH GREEN OLIVES & PRESERVED LEMONS

A tangy Moroccan dish and a regular summer dish on the Leon menu (pictured on page 218).

Feeds: 4
Preparation time: 15 minutes
Cooking time: 30 minutes
✓ WF GF

1 **onion**
2 tablespoons **extra virgin olive oil**
2 cloves of **garlic**
½ teaspoon **ground ginger**
1 teaspoon **ground cumin**
300g **skinless chicken thighs**, on the bone
500ml **chicken stock**
a strand of **saffron**
1 x 240g tin of **chickpeas**
60g **preserved lemon rinds**
50g **pitted green olives**
a small handful of **fresh coriander**
2 tablespoons **crème fraîche**
sea salt and **freshly ground black pepper**

1. Peel and slice the onions and sauté them in the oil in a large saucepan or casserole for a couple of minutes until just soft. Smash and chop the garlic cloves (don't bother to peel them) and add them to the pan with the ground ginger and cumin. Sauté for a few more minutes.

2. Add the chicken thighs, stock, saffron and chickpeas and simmer gently for 10 minutes.

3. Meanwhile slice the preserved lemon rind and destone and halve the olives. Add these to the pan and simmer gently for 5 minutes. Roughly chop the coriander.

4. Add the crème fraîche and coriander and turn the heat up slightly for another 5 minutes, to reduce the sauce. Adjust the seasoning and serve.

TIPS

o You can use left-over chicken from a roast – just add it towards the end of cooking

FRIENDS & FAMILY RECIPES

A gang of us went to Marrakech for the weekend for Greg's 40th, where those who were keen did a day's cookery course at the wonderful Maison Arabe. We cooked this dish, then all sat around the beautiful pool and ate our offerings in the North African sun – heaven!
Apple

Apple and Sophie in Morocco, 2001

My wife Katie is very tolerant about putting up with my nutritional and health adventures. After I suggested we might try and eat less red meat, she was a little concerned about how to satisfy our love of bolognaise… until her friend Robin the weather man suggested that we use turkey instead, saying 'you'd never know the difference'. And he is right.
Well done Robin.
And thank you Katie.
John

TURKEY BOLOGNESE

A great way to use up left-over turkey, and terrific if you are trying to cut back on red meat.

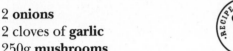

Katie and Natasha in... Turkey

2 **onions**
2 cloves of **garlic**
250g **mushrooms**
2 tablespoons **olive oil**
600g **turkey mince**
1 **dried chilli**
2 x 400g tins of **chopped tomatoes**
2 level tablespoons **tomato purée**
325ml **red wine**
500ml **chicken stock**
a dash of **Worcestershire sauce**
a large sprig of **fresh thyme**
sea salt and **freshly ground black pepper**

1. Peel and finely chop the onions and garlic, and slice the mushrooms.

2. Heat the olive oil in a pan, add the onions and garlic and cook until they are starting to brown. Add the turkey mince and brown it all over, stirring thoroughly to make sure it's cooked throughout.

3. Crumble in the chilli, add the mushrooms, season, and cook for a few minutes.

4. Add the chopped tomatoes, tomato purée, wine, chicken stock, Worcestershire sauce and thyme.

5. Simmer gently on the hob with the lid on for a good hour and a half, making sure it doesn't boil.

TIPS

o   If you are using left-over turkey, grind it into mince in a food processor and add it together with the chilli in step 3.

o   If the bolognese seems to be drying out, add more chicken stock if you have it, or water.

o   After simmering on the hob initially, you can transfer it to an ovenproof dish and cook it in a low oven for an hour, at around 150°C/300°F/gas mark 2.

BEST BOLOGNESE

No freezer should be without a few bags of bolognese. This simple recipe is given real depth of flavour thanks to long cooking and a touch of cinnamon.

3 tablespoons **olive oil**
2 **onions**
4 cloves of **garlic**
200g **streaky bacon** (as fatty as you can find)
1kg **minced beef**
1 x 400g tin of **chopped tomatoes**
½ teaspoon **ground cinnamon**
2 level tablespoons **tomato purée**
500ml **red wine**

1. Heat the oil in a largish saucepan. Finely chop the onions and garlic and add to the pan. Allow to soften for 2 minutes.

2. Chop the bacon into small pieces and add to the pan.

3. When the bacon is starting to go brown at the edges, add the mince and stir to break it up so that it gets browned all over.

4. Add the tinned tomatoes, cinnamon, tomato purée and red wine.

5. Stir, then put a lid on and leave to simmer for 2–3 hours, adding water if necessary to prevent it drying out.

TIPS

o   If I have this on spaghetti, I prefer it with grated Cheddar instead of Parmesan. It reminds me of my 1970s childhood.

o   This is a very versatile dish. Use it to make lasagne. Or stuff courgettes or tomatoes with it and bake in a hot oven for 20 minutes. Slice some potatoes, lay them on top and bake for 30 minutes.

o   The long cooking time is essential to give this dish real depth. Resist the temptation to shorten it too much.

o   A great dish to make in batches of up to four times this amount. Freeze in single portions in small freezer bags.

GILES'S CHOLENT

Henry's friend Giles made this classic Jewish dish a regular weekend feature when his tepid oven only allowed for long slow cooks.

Feeds: 6
Preparation time: 20 minutes + soaking time
Cooking time: 12 hours +
✓ WF DF

approximately 1.5kg **beef brisket**
2 tablespoons **olive oil**
2 large **onions**
6 cloves of **garlic**
170g **pearl barley**
1 tablespoon Hungarian **paprika**
285g **dried haricot beans** (soaked in water for a few hours)
2 tubs of **fresh beef stock**
sea salt and **freshly ground black pepper**

1. In a medium-sized ovenproof casserole, brown the rolled brisket in olive oil then remove it from the pan and put it aside.

2. Peel and slice the onions roughly. Peel the garlic but keep the cloves whole. Put them into the pot and fry until they smell nice.

3. Add the pearl barley and paprika and fry for a minute or two, adding a splash of oil if it all looks stupidly dry.

4. Add the dried haricot beans (soaked for a couple of hours if you remembered). Stir it all about, put the brisket back in and add the beef stock and enough water to cover. Season with salt and pepper.

5. Use a piece of foil under the lid to make a hermetic seal, and place the casserole dish in the oven at around 80–100°C/200°F/gas mark ¼ (or lower) for around 12 hours. Put it in at around midnight and you'll be spot-on for lunch.

6. Remove the lid at the table and you should find the beans and barley cooked (maybe a bit crunchy at the top if there wasn't enough water, though these bits can be stirred in to lend 'complexity'), and the top third of the brisket poking out like a tiny hippo in a swamp, the fat all yellow and yummy-looking. Application of a fork and spoon should pull the meat apart easily.

 **TIPS**

○ Serve up the cholent with lashings of beans and barley and have a jar of pickled cucumbers on the table.

○ Always use Hungarian paprika instead of Spanish, as it retains its red colour and doesn't go brown.

With biblical prohibitions against fire-kindling on the Sabbath, Jewish mothers in the shtetl used to make this dish on Friday before sunset and deliver it to the baker, where it cooked slowly overnight in a warm oven, to be picked up by the husband and children on the way back from shul in the morning. I, however, began cooking it when staying in a cottage in Hawkshead in the Lake District – capital of Wordsworth country – whose only stove was a crap Aga that never got much hotter than a bricky's armpit. I made cholent most weekends, and afterwards would stroll down to the actual synagogue where Wordsworth was barmitzvah'd in 1783.
Giles

FRIENDS & FAMILY
RECIPES

Giles with his sister Victoria, 1975

BRUNO'S OSSO BUCCO

This is a version of the Italian classic, simplified from a recipe by Henry's old boss, chef Bruno Loubet – it's a great party piece to serve if you have friends coming round. (It is fine to eat rose veal, as it comes from the male cows in dairy herds that would otherwise go to waste.)

Feeds: 6
Preparation time: 10 minutes
Cooking time: 2¼ hours
✓ WF DF GF

2 **carrots**
1 **onion**
1 stick of **celery**
2 cloves of **garlic**
3 tablespoons **vegetable oil**
6 slices of **rose veal shank**
1 bottle of **white wine**
200g **plum tomatoes**
8 good-sized **fresh sage leaves**
2 large strips of **orange zest**
sea salt and **freshly ground black pepper**

1. Peel and finely chop the carrots, onions, celery and garlic.

2. Heat the oil in a casserole over a high heat and brown the meat well on both sides (you will need to do this in two or three batches).

3. Remove the meat from the pan, lower the heat then add the vegetables and allow them to colour. Add the meat back to the pan then add the wine.

4. Chop the tomatoes and add them to the pan with the sage and 1 strip of orange zest. Cook on a very low heat for 2 hours, or until the meat is falling off the bone.

5. At this point you can refrigerate the whole thing for up to a week.

6. Remove the meat and vegetables and strain the sauce into a small pan and heat to reduce until lovely and thick. Either plate up the meat and veg and pour over the sauce, or return the meat to the casserole, add the sauce and serve in the pot. Finely chop the remaining strip of orange zest and sprinkle on top for the final touch. You could add chopped parsley too if you like.

TIPS

o The vegetables will be quite well cooked after the 2 hours are up, so some people fry a few more carrots and add them at the end to give a little bite.

o The Italians traditionally serve this with saffron risotto (*risotto Milanese*) and gremolata (chopped parsley, garlic and lemon zest), but it also goes well with mashed potatoes, soft polenta or tagliatelle.

o Serve with a green salad on the side and a good red wine.

FRIENDS & FAMILY
RECIPES

POT ROASTS

Pot-roasting seems too easy to be true. Just put everything into a pot and put the pot into the oven.

The opportunities for experimentation are legion. This section contains a few pot-roasting recipes to get you going, but once you get into the habit you'll find yourself making up new versions all the time. Here are a few tips to help you get the right balance of flavours.

1. What is your theme?
It's a good idea to build your experiments on classic dishes. Classics are classics for a reason – they are combinations that work well together and have been improved upon over the years that they have been handed down. So whether it's a beery English stew or a fruity Moroccan tagine, decide on your theme.

2. How are you going to cook the meat?
Two things to consider here. First, how are you going to brown it? You can do this beforehand by frying it in the pot, or at the end by taking the lid off. Either way, you don't want to miss out on those savoury flavours. Second, are you going to cook it so that it is plump and firm or so it is falling apart? (See Slow Cooking: The Science Bit, page 212.)

3. What is the architecture of the dish?
Think about what vegetables you are going to use and how you are going to chop them. It makes a big difference to the finished result if everything isn't just chopped the same. Also, resist the temptation to throw in too many different vegetables. Keep it simple.

4. What flavours are you going to add to the meat and vegetables?
This could be herbs or spices at the start, or something flavoursome stirred in at the end to perk it up (see the Winter Vegetable Herb Pot Roast on page 241). Be bold.

5. What is providing the sweetness? What is providing the sour?
All great dishes have a balance of sweet and sour. These could come from numerous sources. Good sweeteners include carrots, slow-cooked garlic or onions, dried fruit such as apricots or prunes, beer, pumpkin or sweet potatoes, or simply honey. You can add the sour with vinegar, alcohol (wine, beer, sherry, brandy), citrus or other acidic fruit, tamarind, verjuice (unripened grape juice) and amchoor (a dried powder made from unripe mangoes).

CHICKEN POT ROAST

This is the classic simple supper – pop it all into a large pot when you get home and spend your evening doing something you enjoy.

Feeds: 4
Preparation time: 15 minutes
Cooking time: 1½–2 hours
WF GF DF

5 rashers of **bacon**
500g **carrots**
500g **potatoes**
3 **onions**
1 whole bulb of **garlic**
6 sprigs of **fresh thyme**
2 tablespoons **extra virgin olive oil**
300ml **white wine**
1 whole **chicken**, 1.5–2kg in weight
sea salt and **freshly ground black pepper**

1. Heat the oven to 190°C/375°F/gas mark 5.

2. Roughly chop the bacon. Peel the carrots, but leave the potatoes and onions unpeeled. Roughly chop the carrots and potatoes, and cut the onions into quarters. Cut the unpeeled garlic bulb in half across the middle. Place all these into a casserole with the thyme and seasoning. Add 1 tablespoon of the olive oil and toss thoroughly. Pour in the white wine.

3. Rub the chicken with the remaining tablespoon of olive oil and season well. Place on top of the vegetables.

4. Cook for 1 hour, covered, then remove the lid and cook for another 30 minutes to 1 hour to brown the chicken and, depending on its size, ensure it is cooked through.

TIPS

o This is a very versatile dish. Almost any mix of vegetables, herbs and spices will work as the base. Try thinking in themes: winter pot roast – using root veg and sage; German pot roast – using cabbage, some pieces of sausage and juniper.

o You don't need to stick to chicken. You can use this method with almost any meat – game, beef (particularly the cheap cuts) or lamb. For tougher meats you may need to use more liquid and cook for longer.

o Experiment with the liquid: vermouth, stock and beer all work well.

o If you want something lower GI, replace the potatoes with sweet potatoes.

o If you don't use potatoes, this goes very well with tagliatelle. The combination of the juice and simple buttered pasta is one of life's great pleasures.

o For added zing, blend a handful of soft green herbs, 1 tablespoon of olive oil and 1 clove of garlic to a paste and stir into the vegetables just before serving.

o Try stirring a raw egg yolk into the sauce at the end of cooking to thicken it.

SPANISH POT ROAST

Warm and spicy.

Feeds: 4
Preparation time: 15 minutes
Cooking time: 1½–2 hours
✓ WF DF GF

3 **onions**
3 **carrots**
1 whole bulb of **garlic**
4 **tomatoes**
3 teaspoons **fennel seeds**
2 heaped teaspoons **smoked sweet paprika**
2 tablespoons **olive oil**
1 whole **chicken**, 1.5–2kg in weight
2 tablespoons **sherry vinegar**
250ml **white wine**
sea salt and **freshly ground black pepper**

1. Heat the oven to 190°C/375°F/gas mark 5.

2. Quarter the onions (no need to peel them). Cut the carrots into long batons. Slice the bulb of garlic across and quarter the tomatoes.

3. Put all the vegetables in the bottom of a large casserole with the fennel seeds, 1 tablespoon of the olive oil and 1 teaspoon of the paprika. Season well and stir.

4. Rub the remaining oil and paprika into the chicken along with some salt and pepper. Place the chicken on top of the vegetables and pour in the vinegar and white wine.

5. Cook in the oven for 1 hour, covered, then remove the lid and cook for another 30 minutes to 1 hour to brown the chicken and, depending on its size, ensure it is cooked through.

 TIPS

o Add some peeled potato chunks to the pot for a full meal in one pot.

o Otherwise serve with rice or pasta.

o If you like a bit of spice use hot paprika in place of the sweet stuff.

o Great with some added chunks of chorizo mixed in with the vegetables.

Clockwise from the top (all uncooked): Spanish Pot Roast; Indian Pot Roast Chicken; Pork Belly with Turnips & Prunes

INDIAN POT ROAST CHICKEN

The potatoes in this dish pick up a wonderful lemony, curried flavour (pictured on page 232).

Feeds: 4–6
Preparation time: 15 minutes
Cooking time: 1½–2 hours

WF GF

3 cloves of **garlic**
4 tablespoons **natural yoghurt**
2 teaspoons **turmeric**
2 teaspoons **ground cinnamon**
2 teaspoons **ground coriander**
1 teaspoon **chilli powder**
750g **Charlotte potatoes** or **new potatoes**
1 teaspoon **vegetable oil**
1 **lemon**
1 whole **chicken**, 1.5–2kg in weight
a handful of **fresh coriander leaves**
sea salt and **freshly ground black pepper**

1. Preheat the oven to 190°C/375°F/gas mark 5.

2. Peel and grate the garlic into a bowl, add the yoghurt, spices and chilli and mix well.

3. Slice the unpeeled potatoes fairly thinly and place in a large casserole dish with the oil. Halve the lemon and slice one half finely. Add the lemon slices to the potatoes. Season with salt and pepper.

4. Smear the yoghurt mixture all over the chicken and place it on top of the potatoes. Put the other half of the lemon inside the cavity of the bird.

5. Cook, covered, in the oven for 1 hour, then remove the lid and cook for another 30 minutes to 1 hour to brown the chicken and, depending on its size, ensure it is cooked through.

6. Remove the chicken from the casserole and place on a board. Put the potatoes into a serving dish and sprinkle with the coriander leaves.

 TIPS

- If you don't have the spices you could use a curry paste or powder in their place.

- Also good is to replace the spices with a tablespoon of lime pickle blended finely with the yoghurt.

- To allow the yoghurt and spice mixture to permeate the chicken more, pull the skin away from the breast gently and spread some of the yoghurt underneath the skin.

- Serve with a salad or simple green vegetables.

PORK BELLY WITH TURNIPS AND PRUNES

This dish is so simple to make and so full of flavour (pictured on page 232).

Feeds: 4
Preparation time: 10 minutes
Cooking time: 3 hours
✓ WF DF GF

a chunk of **pork belly** that fits into your casserole, about 1–1.5kg in weight
2 tablespoons **olive oil**
1 **turnip**
2 large **carrots**
1 large **onion**
100g **pitted prunes**
4 **star anise**
15 **coriander seeds**
1 bottle of **white wine** (it's worth it)
sea salt and **freshly ground black pepper**

1. Preheat the oven to 180°C/350°F/gas mark 4.

2. Season the skin of the pork well, then brown it in the olive oil in your casserole. Remove the pork and set aside.

3. Peel the turnip and slice into 5mm rounds. Peel the carrots and cut into batons. Peel and roughly chop the onion. Halve the prunes. Add all the vegetables to the casserole with the prunes and spices.

4. Add the wine, then return the pork to the casserole and put the lid on.

5. Cook for 2½ hours (at least), until the meat is very tender – basting every 30 minutes and adding water if the vegetables dry out too much.

6. Remove the lid and cook for a further 30 minutes.

TIPS

o The vegetables should end up as a glossy thick mixture at the end of cooking.

o You can carefully cut the skin off the pork and roast it in the oven at 200°C/400°F/gas mark 5 for 15 minutes to crisp it up, while the pork stays in the casserole dish.

o If you think the wine is a bit extravagant, you can always replace most of it with chicken stock.

CHICKEN WITH 100 CLOVES OF GARLIC

A pot-roast to show off with, and so simple; the garlic warms and softens and sweetens and creates a lovely depth of flavour..

Feeds: 6
Preparation time: 10 minutes
Cooking time: 1½ hours
✓ WF GF DF

1 medium-sized **chicken**, 1–1.5kg in weight
a glug of **extra virgin olive oil**
3 large handfuls of **fresh thyme**
100 cloves of **garlic** (about 12 bulbs)
200ml **red wine vinegar**
sea salt and **freshly ground black pepper**

1. Preheat the oven to 180°C/350°F/gas mark 4.

2. Smear the chicken with olive oil and plenty of salt and pepper. Break up the garlic bulbs into cloves, but do not peel them.

3. Stuff the chicken with the thyme and about 20 cloves of garlic. Place the rest of the garlic in a casserole and nestle the chicken on top. Pour in the vinegar.

4. Cover and cook for approximately 1 hour, adding up to 200ml of water if necessary to stop it drying out.

5. Remove the lid and cook for a further 30 minutes to brown the chicken.

TIPS

o Serve with tagliatelle and a green salad with balsamic dressing (see page 163).

o Try squeezing the roasted garlic from its skin and spread it on bread with a little salt: a delicious way to use up the garlic which will be left over.

When John and I came to write our list of recipes for the book this dish was on both our lists. This dish is a good example of how recipes are passed down through the generations. When I showed the recipe to my mum, she told me that it was a dish that her mother used to make, but in the old French tradition with 100 bulbs (rather than cloves) of garlic. That must have been quite something.
Henry

This has big memories for me. It is the first thing I ever cooked – for a girlfriend when I was fourteen. The recipe was given to me by my Auntie Nita. In retrospect, not a good dinner for a date…
John

Leon, Nita, Tim, Marion and Joe in Portugal 1965

RIGAS'S LAMB

This dish was made for us by our (Greek) friend Dimitri, from a recipe that has been handed down in his family for generations.

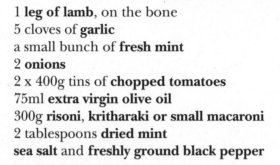

Rigas (left) with Chloe, Dimitri and Dan, Antiparos, Cyclades

FRIENDS & FAMILY RECIPES

Feeds: 6–8
Preparation time: 20 minutes
Cooking time: 3½ hours
DF

1 **leg of lamb**, on the bone
5 cloves of **garlic**
a small bunch of **fresh mint**
2 **onions**
2 x 400g tins of **chopped tomatoes**
75ml **extra virgin olive oil**
300g **risoni, kritharaki or small macaroni**
2 tablespoons **dried mint**
sea salt and **freshly ground black pepper**

1. Preheat the oven to 150°C/300°F/gas mark 2.

2. With the tip of a sharp knife, make 6 or 7 quite deep holes on both sides of the meat. Stuff these with small pieces of garlic, followed by an equal amount of salt and black pepper mixed together. Plug the holes with a couple of leaves of fresh mint, and season the meat with a little more salt and pepper.

3. Finely chop the onions and put them into a large roasting dish. Add the tomatoes and oil and stir well. Put the meat on top, and place in the oven.

4. Cook for 3½ hours. Keep adding water to the sauce to prevent it from drying out. If you like, you can baste the lamb with spoonfuls of the sauce so that it forms a crust of caramelized onions on the meat.

5. When 20 minutes of cooking time is left, add a cup of water to the sauce and stir in the risoni or macaroni.

6. Season, sprinkle well with dried mint (use more than you think you should – it adds a peppery kick to the sauce) and put back into the oven until the pasta is tender. The risoni will expand and absorb the liquid sauce, which in turn will have absorbed all the juices from the meat. Keep adding water and stirring every 5–10 minutes if you need to so that the pasta stays moist and doesn't stick.

TIPS

o To serve, try green beans, allowed to cool slightly and sprinkled with lemon juice, olive oil and salt and pepper. Otherwise a green or Greek salad makes a good accompaniment.

Rigas is my dad. Dad and his parents came to Britain as refugees from the Greek civil war in the Forties. This recipe comes originally from his mum Vivi, who died while he was just a young man. On the little Greek island where dad's family house is still located, most people did not have gas ovens in their homes when I was a kid. My early memories of being there are of watching families walking through the village on Sundays with huge trays of lamb, pork or stuffed tomatoes carried aloft; they were all heading to the bakery that had the only big ovens on the island, and which became a communal kitchen every weekend and feast day. Cooking this dish at home in London brings to mind whitewashed houses with blue shutters, the sound of crickets beating in the heat and the strange sweet drinks that came out of a dispenser in the bakery. *Dimitri*

WINTER VEGETABLE HERB POT ROAST

A great way to use up ungainly winter vegetables. The trick is the flash of raw garlic and parsely at the end which lifts everything.

Feeds: 4–6
Preparation time: 15 minutes
Cooking time: 1½ hours
♥ ✓ WF DF GF V

For the pot
2 **onions**
4 **parsnips**
1 **butternut squash**
3 **carrots**
a large handful of **fresh sage**
2 tablespoons **extra virgin olive oil**
1 glass of **white wine**
1 x 400g tin of **flageolet beans**
sea salt and **freshly ground black pepper**

To finish
3 cloves of **garlic**
a handful of **fresh flat-leaf parsley**
a dash of **olive oil**

1. Preheat the oven to 200°C/400°F/gas mark 6.

2. Peel and slice the onions. Peel the parsnips and quarter them lengthways. Deseed the butternut squash and cut it into large chunks (leaving the skin on). Peel the carrots and slice them diagonally. Roughly chop the sage.

3. Put all the vegetables, except the beans, into a casserole dish with the olive oil, white wine and sage. Cook in the oven for 1 hour with the lid on.

4. Add the drained beans and cook for another 30 minutes with the lid off. You may want to add a little water if it gets too dry.

5. Just before serving, blitz the garlic with the parsley and a little olive oil. Season and stir into the casserole.

TIPS

○ You can use any combination of winter vegetables – celeriac, pumpkin, potatoes, shallots, celery, turnips, swede, beetroot, all work well.

○ Don't be afraid to mix in a few greens – kale, cabbage, winter and spring greens will all be happy in the pot.

○ Try popping in a few chestnuts.

BOIL OR BAKE IN THE BAG

The seventies. The decade of space-age convenience food. Smash, Pot Noodle, Angel Delight. Suddenly, all our meals had to be freeze-dried and reconstituted, as if we had turned into a nation of astronauts.

And then there's boil-in-a-bag: a seventies invention that has turned into a culinary classic. Often used by Michelin-starred chefs these days, it is one of the easiest ways to speedily prepare a quick supper or a full-on dinner party.

Clockwise from top: Sea Bass with Thai Spices; Quail with Thyme & Garlic; Mackerel with Rosemary & Flageolets, all before cooking

QUAIL *with thyme & garlic*

Feeds: 2, as a starter
Preparation time: 15 minutes
Cooking time: 1½ hours

✓ WF GF

2 **quails**
1 tablespoon **olive oil**
½ a small **onion**
3 cloves of **garlic**
25g **butter**
1 large bunch of **fresh thyme**
80ml **chicken stock** (made with ¼ of a stock cube if you don't have fresh stock)
4 tablespoons **brandy**
juice of 1 **lemon**
sea salt and **freshly ground black pepper**

1. Preheat the oven to 180°C/350°F/gas mark 4.

2. Season the quails well with salt and pepper. Heat the olive oil in a frying pan and brown the quails, breast side down.

3. Cut two rectangles of foil large enough to encase the quails, lay them on top of each other and place on a baking tray. Place the browned quails in the middle of the foil, with their legs interlocking.

4. Very finely dice the onion and garlic and sprinkle on top with the butter and thyme. Draw up the foil round each side and pour in the stock, brandy and lemon juice.

5. Seal the foil up as tightly as you can and pop into the oven for 2 hours.

6. When the time is up, carefully open the parcel. If the sauce is still liquid, pour it into a small pan and boil it down until reduced. Serve the sauce with the quails.

TIPS

○ Serve with celeriac boiled in milk till soft and blitzed with butter and nutmeg.

○ If you can't find quails, this works just as well with chicken thighs on the bone.

○ As with all 'foiled' dishes, you can get them ready for the oven a day in advance.

MACKEREL *with rosemary & flageolets*

Feeds: 4
Preparation time: 15 minutes
Cooking time: 30 minutes

♥ ✓ WF GF DF

½ a bulb of **fennel**
1 **carrot**
½ a **red onion**
1 x 290g tin of **flageolet beans**
olive oil
2 whole **mackerel** or 4 **mackerel fillets**
a big sprig of **fresh rosemary**
200ml **white wine**
sea salt and **freshly ground black pepper**

1. Preheat the oven to 220°C/425°F/gas mark 7.

2. Chop the fennel and carrot into very fine strips and slice the onion finely. The vegetables must all be cut nice and fine or they will not cook. Drain and rinse the flageolet beans.

3. Tear off 2 pieces of foil big enough to enclose the mackerel, lay them on top of each other and place on a baking tray. Oil the centre of the foil with a little olive oil.

4. Lay the mackerel (skin side down if using fillets) on the foil. Sprinkle over the fennel, carrot and onion, and add the rosemary.

5. Scatter over the beans, season, and draw up the foil round the sides, leaving a pouring vent in the middle at the top. Pour in the white wine, seal the parcel well, and place in the oven for 30 minutes.

TIPS

Works well with any robust fish.

o Cannellini, butter beans and borlotti work as well as flageolets.

SEA BASS *with Thai spices*

Feeds: 2
Preparation time: 10 minutes
Cooking time: 20 minutes
♥ ✓ WF GF DF

1 teaspoon **sesame oil**
2 fillets of **sea bass**
a 2.5cm piece of **fresh ginger**
1 clove of **garlic**
½ a **fresh red chilli**
2 **spring onions**
1 tablespoon **fish sauce**
2 tablespoons **white wine**
1 tablespoon **soy sauce**

1. Preheat the oven to 220°C/425°F/gas mark 7.

2. Tear off 2 rectangles of foil big enough to encase the fish, lay them on top of each other and place on a baking tray. Lightly oil the centre of the foil with the oil.

3. Lay the fish fillets skin side down on the foil.

4. Peel the ginger and garlic. Deseed the chilli. Chop them all finely. Cut the spring onions into long diagonals. Sprinkle the ginger, garlic, chilli and spring onions over the fish.

5. Draw up the foil round each side and pour over the fish sauce, wine and soy sauce and seal up the foil as tightly as you can. Put into the oven and cook for 20 minutes.

TIPS

o Great with basmati rice or rice noodles. If you want to make this a meal in a bag, you could add a handful of tinned cannellini beans to the foil before you seal it up.

FRIDGE RAIDERS

Provider of the fastest food in the world: the fridge. There for us in the morning, when we get back from work and in the middle of the night.

This section is about knowing what to feed your old friend so that it can feed you.

These recipes can sit a while without suffering from the cold. Some of them – Scotch eggs, say – are so easy to buy that you might never have thought of making your own. But the recipes are simple and fun, your friends will be disproportionately impressed, and you can be confident that no nasties have found their way into the finished product.

Henry's fridge, including Spicy Chicken Drumsticks, Ginger Chilli Prawns, Roasted Artichokes and Scotch Eggs

GINGER & CHILLI PRAWNS

Feeds: 2
Preparation time: 5 minutes
Cooking time: 5 minutes
♥ ✓ WF DF GF

1 fresh **red chilli**
a 2.5cm piece of **fresh ginger**
10 large raw peeled **prawns**
1 tablespoon **extra virgin olive oil**
sea salt and **freshly ground black pepper**

This dish scores well on ease, theatre and flavour. Cook this when you want to be on a beach in India without having to leave the house. It's tempting to have one hot before leaving the rest to cool and wait for you in the fridge.
John

1. Deseed the chilli and peel the ginger. Slice them both into fine strips.

2. Shallow-fry everything in the olive oil until the prawns are cooked and turn pink.

3. Season with salt and pepper and serve.

 TIPS

○ If you want to cheat buy cooked prawns, already shelled, and flash fry them for 2 minutes to heat through. You can also use dried chilli flakes or powder. It's still best to use fresh ginger, though.

○ Be careful to check on the provenance of your prawns when you buy them. You can now get sustainable ones from the North Atlantic.

SPICY CHICKEN DRUMSTICKS

These could not be more simple. A perfect thing to store in the fridge to pick on when hunger strikes at strange times.

Feeds: 4
Preparation time: 3 minutes
Cooking time: 45 minutes
✓ WF GF DF

8 **chicken drumsticks**
1 tablespoon **extra virgin olive oil**
1 tablespoon runny **honey**
2 teaspoons **mild curry powder**
½ a **lemon**
sea salt and **freshly ground black pepper**

1. Preheat the oven to 240°C/475°F/gas mark 9.

2. Lay a sheet of foil in a baking tray, leaving a little excess sticking up around the sides.

3. With a sharp knife slash the sides of the chicken drumsticks – this will allow the flavours to seep in and the meat to cook evenly.

4. Put the chicken in a bowl and add the oil, honey and curry powder and mix well to coat the chicken. Then tip the chicken onto the baking tray and add some salt and pepper. Pop into the oven for 45 minutes, turning the drumsticks every 15 minutes or so.

5. Take out of the oven, leave to cool for a few minutes, then douse with a squeeze of lemon.

MARION'S SCOTCH EGGS

Best hot from the pan, but also a great fridge raider.

Feeds: 6
Preparation time: 20 minutes
Cooking time: 15 minutes
✓ DF

6 **eggs**
500g **sausage meat**
2 teaspoons **English mustard**
2 handfuls of **fresh breadcrumbs**
4 tablespoons **vegetable oil**
sea salt and **freshly ground black pepper**

John and his mum, 1972

FRIENDS & FAMILY RECIPES

IMMEDIATE

My mum Marion (Leon's wife) is in my book the mistress of Scotch eggs. We would either eat them warm, (lovely), or take them to the Essex coast (Tollesbury) on weekend-trips. I still don't know whether they are best eaten whole (in many bites not all at once) or cut in half. The only solution is to have two – one whole, one cut in two. *John*

1. Hard-boil the eggs, then shell them and dry with kitchen paper.

2. Season the meat with salt and pepper and add the mustard.

3. Using wet hands, divide the sausage meat into 6 egg-sized balls. Spread the breadcrumbs in a dish.

4. Take a ball of sausage meat and spread it out into a disc in the palm of your hand. Lay an egg on it and gently work the sausage meat until it smoothly encases the egg. Drop it into the breadcrumbs and roll it around until covered.

5. Heat the oil in a pan and gently fry the Scotch eggs until golden brown all over.

RECIPE TESTED BY KATE

TIPS

○ Try making variations by mixing some black pudding or chorizo into the meat.

○ If you want to show off, boil the eggs so that the yolks are still slightly soft.

○ You could use duck's or quail's eggs to make alternative sized Scotch eggs. A hot Scotch duck egg with a little green salad makes the smartest starter you could imagine.

○ Some books will tell you to deep fry them – no, no, we disagree.

ROASTED TINNED ARTICHOKES

Preparation time: 1 minute
Cooking time: 10 minutes
♥ ✓ WF DF GF V

1 tin or tub of **artichoke hearts in oil**
extra **olive oil**, if necessary

1. Preheat the oven to 200°C/400°F/gas mark 6.

2. Arrange the artichokes on a baking tray or in an oven dish. If they have not been previously kept in oil, brush them liberally with olive oil.

3. Put into the oven for 10 minutes.

4. Store on a plate in the fridge for when hunger strikes.

TIPS

○ You can griddle the artichokes on the hob if you prefer.

RECIPE TESTED BY PETA

PRESERVED FLAVOURS

People have always needed to preserve their food, especially in countries where winter can spell famine. The autumn glut of fruit and vegetables had to be made to last until spring. Any surplus livestock – too costly to keep alive over winter – would be butchered and then salted, smoked or potted. Great ribbons of sausages would hang from the rafters. Strong fingers would tie hams to pegs driven into soft chimney brick.

Preservation techniques take their cue from the climate. In the damp forests of northern Europe, unsuitable for sun- or wind-drying, we have relied largely on fermenting, pickling, smoking, salting and (more recently, after sugar started coming to us from the West Indies) sugaring.

These techniques have helped define national palates. We love our pickles and our cheeses. The Portuguese write ballads to their bacalhau (salt cod). The Germans pile their fermented cabbage (sauerkraut) high with salted sausages. In Sweden, surströmming – fermented fish – was developed at a time when salting was too expensive. It continues to ferment in its tins, which develop a distinctive bulge over time. Henry's grandfather developed a taste for the stuff when he was a diplomat in Sweden. He was exiled to the garden to eat it. Even there, an ominous hiss as the opener pierced the pregnant tin would be followed by a release of a gas so vile that the neighbours would often complain.

These days – when we can buy anything we want, whenever we want – we tend to view preserving as a form of experimental cooking, for those with time on their hands. But it can be much more than that. Not only does it create bold-flavoured morsels that can be eaten when you have less time on your hands – it is also a great way to get in touch with your culinary roots.

PICKLING

Time was when the onset of autumn – the glut of the harvest, with the promise of winter famine to come – would be greeted by a frenzy of pickling. Preserving vegetables in vinegar (rather than salt) made sense in northern countries, where beer (and its close relation, malt vinegar) was cheap and abundant.

Vinegar also has the advantage that you don't need to soak the salt out of the vegetables before eating them. And they retain a satisfyingly fresh crunch. If necessity is the mother of invention, the pickle is one of her most talented offspring.

PICKLING *by Katie*

This year has been a revelation. We've moved to the country. We have a garden, in which things grow. Some of them I recognize, and have even planted, but others have been a wonderful, confusing and glut-inducing mystery. Call it work ethic, call it guilt, but I can't bear the idea of waste. Especially if Mother Nature's been good enough to provide me with loads and loads of sometimes ugly but free and tasty fruit and veg. And so my voyage into the world of pickles, chutneys, jellies and jams has begun. I've had to read a lot of books, and talk to lots of friends' aunties. I've bought a really massive preserving pan, and a jelly bag. I've discovered the wonders of websites like Lakeland. And after considerable trial and error, and some really nasty episodes with burnt sugar (and burnt tongues), I've had the satisfaction of sticking labels on jars and filling up a shelf in the larder with stuff I've made. From our garden.

Katie's top tips for making chutney

o The ratio of fruit/vegetables : vinegar : sugar will vary depending on the sweetness and acidity of the fruit and vegetables, but as a rule of thumb you can start with 3kg : 1 litre : 500g and adjust for taste. Don't be frightened and feel tied to recipes; the beauty of chutney is that you can use almost any fruit or vegetable, and experiments with spices work.

o It is worth buying a really good, big preserving (maslin) pan. It gives an even heat for those 3-hour simmers, and feels very Mrs Beeton.

o Don't shred your fruit and veg too fine, as you'll end up with a spicy purée, but neither be TOO slapdash with your chopping. Just think about having half an onion falling out of your cheese and pickle sandwich. Keep those pieces bite-sized.

Above (blue plate): Jossy's Onion, Orange & Sweet Pepper Chutney; Middle left: Katie's Posh Onion Marmalade; Middle right: Claudia's Aubergine Pickle; Below: Katie's 'Chuck-it-all-in Chutney'

KATIE'S 'CHUCK-IT-ALL-IN CHUTNEY'

Makes: 6–8 jars, depending on size
Preparation time: 30 minutes
Cooking time: 3–4 hours
♥ DF V

My father-in-law, Leon (yes, that one), went into the greenhouse at the end of September and picked all the green tomatoes. 'There you are,' he said. 'Now you can make chutney.' *Katie*

2 kg **green tomatoes** or ripe **red tomatoes**
450g **onions**
450g **apples**
6 **plums**
2 fresh **green chillies**
255g **raisins** or **currants**, or a mixture
1 level tablespoon **salt**
450g **brown sugar**
6 cloves of **garlic**
a 5cm piece of **fresh ginger**
2 **cinnamon sticks**
10 **cloves**
1.2 litres **malt vinegar**, or any other vinegar

1. Chop the tomatoes and onions finely. Core the apples and stone the plums, then chop finely (you can leave the skins on the apples). Deseed and chop the chillies.

2. Put all the chopped fruit, vegetables and chillies into a big pan, along with the raisins or currants, salt and sugar. Crush the garlic and add to the pan. Stir well.

3. Wrap the ginger and spices in a muslin square, or an old tea towel, and tie with string, leaving the ends long enough to tie to the pan handle so that the bundle can be removed easily. (Or you can use a 'pickling basket' if you have one.) Add your spice bundle to the pan with the vinegar.

4. Bring to the boil, then reduce the heat and let the chutney simmer very gently for about 3 hours. Stir occasionally. You'll know the consistency is about right when you can drag a spoon through the mixture and it leaves a trail that doesn't immediately fill up with vinegar.

5. Pour the hot chutney into hot jars (you can't skimp on the sterilizing bit, see below). Cover the chutney with a disc of waxed paper, wax side down, and seal tightly with a lid.

6. Label when it's cold, and DON'T EAT IT for AT LEAST a month, preferably two. The flavours mellow, and it's much more delicious. It will keep for at least a year, sealed. Once you've opened it, keep it in the fridge.

How to sterilize jars for chutneys and jams:

Put clean, washed and dried jam jars or bottles into a cold oven with the lids off.

Turn the oven on to 160°C/325°F/ gas mark 3 and put the timer on for 20 minutes.

When the timer goes, turn off the oven leaving the jars inside to cool slightly.

Pour in the jam, jelly, chutney or syrup while the jars are still hot.

FRIENDS & FAMILY RECIPES

CLAUDIA'S AUBERGINE PICKLE (Brinjal Kasaundi)

A sensational pickle to serve with curries, with left over rice or cold meat.

Makes: 1 large jar
Preparation time: 10 minutes
Cooking time: 40 minutes
♥ WF DF GF V

1kg **aubergines**
1 **fresh red chilli**, deseeded
a 5cm piece of **fresh ginger**
8 cloves of **garlic**
1 tablespoon **ground cumin**
250ml **wine vinegar**
250ml **toasted sesame oil**
1 tablespoon **mustard seeds**
1 teaspoon **fenugreek seeds**
6 **curry leaves**
1 teaspoon **turmeric**
100g **sugar**
sea salt

1. First, sterilize your jars (see page 254).

2. Cut the aubergines into 1.5cm slices. Blend the chilli, ginger, garlic and cumin with a little of the vinegar in a food processor.

3. Heat 3 tablespoons of the oil in a large pan and add the mustard and fenugreek seeds. When they start to crackle, add the curry leaves along with the ginger and chilli paste. Cook until the mixture becomes a golden colour.

4. Add the turmeric, sugar and remaining vinegar and stir well. Add the aubergines, season with salt and bring to the boil. Simmer gently for about 30 minutes.

5. Allow the mixture to cool, then pour it into a jar. Cover with the remaining oil. This will keep for a few months in the fridge.

TIPS

o Depending on the size of your jar, you may need to add a little more oil to cover the aubergines.

Claudia Roden has been a friend of my mother since I was a child. She has an encyclopedic knowledge of Middle Eastern and Mediterranean food, which she passes on with a gentle and warm enthusiasm. She is also a spectacular cook. We have a test at Leon when we are devising dishes for the menu: would we be proud to serve it to Claudia?
This recipe is one she found in the Bene Israel Jewish community in India, and first appeared in
The Book of Jewish Food. If you have never used any of her cookbooks, you have a treat in store.
Henry

FRIENDS & FAMILY RECIPES

Claudia Roden

JOSSY'S ONION, ORANGE & SWEET PEPPER CHUTNEY

Makes: 3 large jars
Preparation time: 40 minutes
Cooking time: 1 hour 15 minutes
♥ WF DF GF V

2 fresh **red chillies**
6 cloves of **garlic**
a 5cm piece of **fresh ginger**
3 large **onions**
1 large **orange pepper**
3 large **oranges**
10 **cardamom pods**
1 teaspoon **turmeric**
2 teaspoons **black onion seeds**
225g **granulated sugar**
300ml **white wine vinegar**
sea salt

1. First, sterilize your jars
   (see page 254).

2. Deseed and slice the
   chillies, and peel and finely
   slice the garlic and ginger.

3. Peel the onions and cut into quarters, then
   slice finely. Deseed the pepper and cut into
   fairly small pieces.

4. Squeeze the orange juice into a heavy pan.
   Scrape the pith out of the orange halves and
   discard, then cut the skins into small pieces
   and add to the pan with the chillies and garlic.

5. Lightly crush the cardamom pods and add to the
   pan with the turmeric, onion seeds, sugar, vinegar
   and 300ml of water. Season with salt, stir well and
   bring the mixture to the boil. Simmer as gently
   as you can, uncovered, for about 1 hour,
   stirring occasionally.

6. Pour into jars when cool and store in the fridge.
   It will keep for 6 months unopened.

KATIE'S POSH ONION MARMALADE

This is a bit classier than the Chuck-it-all-in Chutney, and doesn't take as long to make. But you have to keep it in the fridge. It's inspired by Sarah Raven's fantastic *Garden Cookbook*.

Makes: 2 small jars
Preparation time: 10 minutes
Cooking time: 40 minutes
♥ WF DF GF V

450g **onions**
2 cloves of **garlic**
olive oil
4 tablespoons **red wine**
4 tablespoons **balsamic vinegar**
1 tablespoon **soft brown sugar**
1 sprig of **fresh thyme**
sea salt and **freshly ground black pepper**

1. First, sterilize your jars (see page 254).

2. Slice the onions finely, and crush the garlic.

3. Heat the olive oil in a heavy-bottomed pan, and gently cook the onion and garlic for 20 minutes, being careful not to let them brown.

4. Add the wine, vinegar and sugar, and simmer very slowly until most of the liquid has gone.

5. Add the thyme, salt and pepper, and cook for a few more minutes. You can leave the thyme in if you've stripped the leaves and chopped them. If you just dropped the stalks in whole, for flavour, take them out.

6. Pour into hot sterilized jars and seal. This will keep in the fridge for a month or two.

FRIENDS & FAMILY RECIPES

JOJO'S LEMON & UGLY LIME MARMALADE

Jojo Tulloh is our gardening guru and author of the wonderful *Freshly Picked*. She often gives this as a Christmas present to people who love home-made marmalade. They will usually have run out by then and be suffering marmalade withdrawal while waiting for the new season's Sevilles to arrive in mid-January.

Jojo in her allotment, summer 2009

Makes: 5 large jars
Preparation time: 30 minutes
Cooking time: 2 hours
♥ WF DF GF V

6 **lemons**
2 round **Indian green limes**
2 yellow **grapefruit**
1 **ugly lime**, or kaffir limes as they are commonly known
2.5kg **unbleached granulated sugar**

1. Scrub the lemons and green limes and cut them in half. Squeeze the juice into a jug and keep the pips. Set the jug of juice aside. Cut the skins into thin julienne strips and place in a preserving pan.

2. Peel the skin from the grapefruit and the ugly lime with a potato peeler. Cut the pith from the grapefruit flesh, remove and keep any pips and put the flesh into the pan. Put the peeled ugly lime, all the pips and the pith into a muslin jelly bag and tie up with string.

3. Chop the grapefruit and ugly lime skins into thin strips and add to the pan with 3 litres of water and the jelly bag. Simmer gently for 1½ hours. When the peel is soft, take the jelly bag out and squeeze it to get all the juice out into the pan (this will help the marmalade set).

4. Put a couple of saucers into the freezer. Measure the mixture in the pan and add 450g of sugar for every 500ml of mixture. Then add the reserved lemon and lime juice and put the pan on a low heat.

5. Bring to a simmer until the sugar has dissolved, then boil rapidly. After 15 minutes start testing to see if your marmalade is ready – it shouldn't take longer than 45 minutes. (Test this by taking a saucer out of the freezer. Put a teaspoon of marmalade on the saucer, wait a minute, then push the mixture with your finger. If it wrinkles, your marmalade has reached setting point.)

6. Let the marmalade cool for 30 minutes, stirring occasionally, then pour into your warm sterilized jars (see page 254 for tips on sterilizing your jars).

FRIENDS & FAMILY RECIPES

Ramekin above: Blackberry Compote
Middle: Strawberry Compote
Below: Jojo's Lemon & Ugly Lime Marmalade

JOSSY'S FRESH APRICOT & CITRUS JAM *with pine nuts*

This heavenly jam is wonderful stirred into natural yoghurt – or spread on toast or croissants for breakfast or tea, of course. As with everything, this is best made in season.

Makes: 6 x 500g jars
Preparation time: 10 minutes
Cooking time: 25–30 minutes
♥ WF GF DF V

1.75kg large **fresh apricots**
300ml **fresh orange juice**
5 tablespoons **lemon juice**
1.75g **preserving sugar with pectin**
50g **pine nuts**
15g **unsalted butter**
3–4 teaspoons **apricot brandy** – optional

1. First, sterilize your jars (see page 254).

2. Meanwhile halve the apricots and put them into a preserving pan, discarding the stones. Pour the orange juice into a measuring jug, add the lemon juice and bring the total amount of liquid up to 450ml with water.

3. Add the liquid to the apricots. Put the pan over a high heat, bring to the boil, then lower the heat and simmer gently for 10–15 minutes, or until the apricots are soft but not mushy.

4. Remove the pan from the heat and add the sugar, stirring until it dissolves.

5. Heat a dry frying pan and toss the pine nuts around for a minute or two to brown. Add them to the pan with the butter. Return the pan to a high heat, bring the jam to the boil and boil rapidly for 4–5 minutes. Spoon off any scum that rises to the top.

6. Add the apricot brandy if using, and leave the jam to settle for 15 minutes before potting. Remove the hot jars from the oven and ladle the jam into them. Cover each one first with a waxed disc, then with a lid or cellophane. After opening a jar, it's a good idea to keep it in the fridge. It should keep for a good 4 months.

STRAWBERRY COMPOTE

Makes: 350ml, feeds: 4
Preparation time: 2 minutes
Cooking time: 20 minutes
♥ ✓ WF GF DF V

350g **strawberries**, frozen or fresh
juice of ½ a **lemon**
1 tablespoon + 1 teaspoon **fructose**

1. Combine all the ingredients in a small, heavy-based pan with a lid.

2. Bring the ingredients to a gentle boil and allow to bubble for 5 minutes, then remove the lid.

3. Simmer for a further 15 minutes, or until the fruit has collapsed and the sauce is thickish – it will thicken as it cools. Pour into jars and serve, or store in the fridge.

PETRA'S QUINCE JELLY

Perfect on toast, with cheese, with cold left-over meat, with everything.

Makes: 6 medium jars
Preparation time: 10 minutes
Cook time: 2 hours
♥ WF GF DF V

1.4kg **quinces**
450g **apples**
granulated sugar
2 **lemons**

Petra and Jeremy in the Hebrides, June 1967

RECIPE TESTED BY JEREMY

1. Wash the quinces well to remove any fuzz on the skin, then cut the quinces and apples into small pieces, but do not peel or remove the cores.

2. Place in a preserving pan and cover with water. Put a lid on the pan, or cover with foil to prevent evaporation, and simmer gently until tender; this may take up to 2 hours.

3. Pour the contents of the pan into a jelly bag and leave for 12 hours, suspended over a bowl. To each 600ml of juice add 450g of sugar and the juice of ½ a lemon.

4. Bring the liquid to the boil, then leave to boil gently until it sets – it should take about 20 minutes (see page 259 for tips on setting).

5. Pour into hot sterilized jars and put jam pot covers on immediately. It will keep for 6 months unopened in the fridge.

My mother and father-in-law dedicate months (or so it seems) every year to dealing with the glut of quinces that grow in their London garden. They have cooked every possible recipe that involves quinces, but this jelly is always the number one. Family members beg to have their quotas increased. *Henry*

BLACKBERRY COMPOTE & SPICES

An autumnal compote with a warm spiciness. A staple on the Leon menu.

Feeds: 4
Preparation time: 2 minutes
Cooking time: 20 minutes
♥ ✓ WF DF GF V

300g **blackberries**, frozen or fresh
juice of ¼ of a **lemon**
2 tablespoons **fructose**
a pinch of **ground cinnamon**
a pinch of **ground star anise**

RECIPE TESTED BY EMMA

1. Simply combine all the ingredients in a small, heavy-based pan and cover with a lid.

2. Bring to a gentle boil, and after 5 minutes remove the lid.

3. Simmer for another 15 minutes, until the fruit has collapsed and the sauce is thickish – it will thicken as it cools. Pour into sterilized jars and serve or store in the fridge.

TIPS

o Great in natural yoghurt, on toast, on ice cream, on porridge. We could go on.

o Will keep in the fridge for weeks.

POTTING

The precursor of canning and vacuum-packing, potting is one of the simplest ways to preserve food. It works by killing off any bacteria contained within the food and then shutting out the germs.

Its major advantage from a gastronomic perspective is that the barrier used to shut out the germs tends to be a flavour-rich layer of fat. Yum.

As a quick lunch, it is hard to better some hot toast topped with a little terrine or potted meat from this section and a smear of pickle from the last. Heaven.

POTTED MEATS

A great way to use up left-over roasts of any kind – spread on sourdough toast and served with a little chutney.

Feeds: 2–4
Preparation time: 10 minutes
Cooking time: 5 minutes
+ 1 hour to set
✓ WF GF

100g **unsalted butter**
1 **bay leaf**
150g cold **cooked meat**
½ teaspoon **cayenne**
zest of 1 **lemon**
a good scratch of **nutmeg**
sea salt and **freshly ground black pepper**

1. Put the butter and the bay leaf into a small pan and place over a gentle heat until the butter has melted.

2. Take the cold meat and chop it up finely. Put it into a bowl and stir in the butter (as you pour the butter in you can leave the watery deposit at the bottom of the pan, effectively clarifying it). Remove and reserve the bay leaf.

3. Add the lemon zest, nutmeg and cayenne and season well with salt and pepper.

4. Mix well, then put into a small dish or jar, squashing the meat down so that it is all coated in butter. Put the bay leaf on top and leave in the fridge for an hour or so to set. It will keep for a month in the fridge.

JOHN BUCHAN'S TERRINE

A simple terrine, perfect with a bit of strong chutney.

Feeds: 8–10
Preparation time: 30 minutes
Cooking time: 1½ hours
✓ WF GF

12 rashers of **smoked streaky bacon**
1 small **onion**
500g **pork belly**
300g **pork loin steaks**
1 teaspoon **ground coriander**
2 **eggs**
50ml **double cream**
250ml white wine
sea salt and **cracked black pepper**

1. Preheat the oven to 180°C/350°F/gas mark 4.

2. Line a 25cm long terrine dish with the bacon, leaving any excess hanging over the edge. Finely chop the onion.

3. Carefully remove the skin from the pork belly (you can oil and salt it, then roast it in a high oven for 90 minutes to make scratchings). Cube the belly flesh and the pork loin and put them into a food processor with the onion, coriander, eggs and cream. Pour in the white wine and 3 healthy pinches of sea salt and some pepper. Now blend everything together until you have little pea-sized pieces of meat.

4. Put the mixture into the terrine and flip the excess streaky bacon over the top. Put the terrine into a deep oven tray and pour water into the tray so that it comes halfway up the sides of the terrine.

5. Cook in the oven for 1½ hours, uncovered, then remove and leave to cool at room temperature before serving.

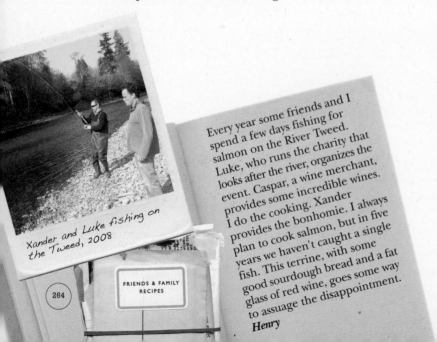

Xander and Luke fishing on the Tweed, 2008

FRIENDS & FAMILY RECIPES

Every year some friends and I spend a few days fishing for salmon on the River Tweed. Luke, who runs the charity that looks after the river, organizes the event. Caspar, a wine merchant, provides some incredible wines. I do the cooking. Xander provides the bonhomie. I always plan to cook salmon, but in five years we haven't caught a single fish. This terrine, with some good sourdough bread and a fat glass of red wine, goes some way to assuage the disappointment.
Henry

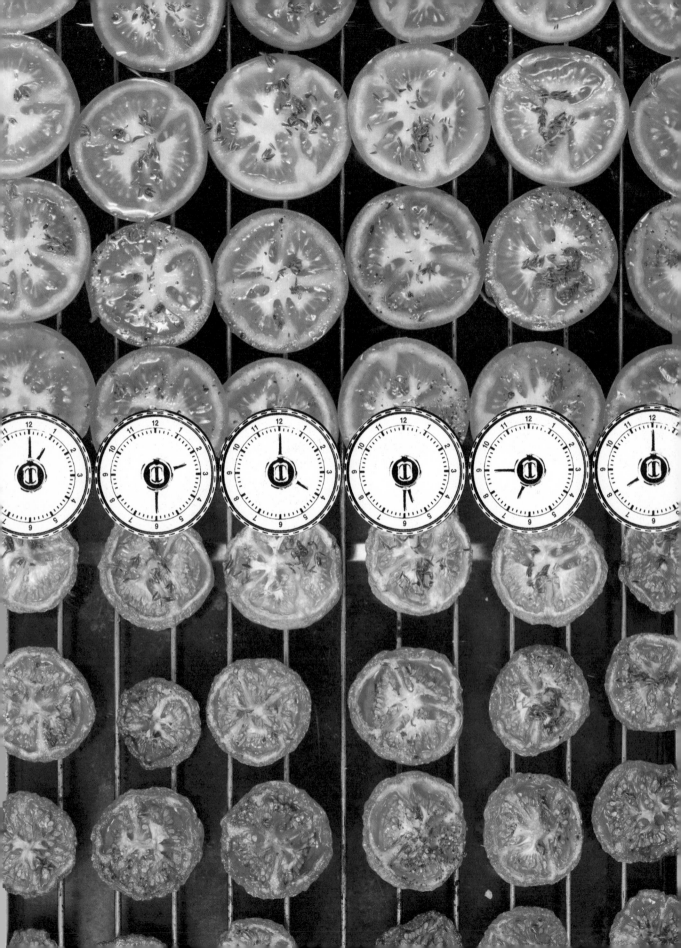

'SUN-DRIED' TOMATOES

These 'sun-dried' tomatoes taste far fresher than shop-bought ones, and are really simple to make. Once you have got the hang of making them, you will never go back.

Makes: 1 medium kilner jar
Preparation time: 5 minutes
Cooking time: 7 hours
♥ ✓ WF DF GF V

500g **tomatoes**
2 teaspoons **sea salt**
1 teaspoon **freshly ground black pepper**
a sprig of **fresh thyme**
olive oil
1 clove of **garlic**

1. Preheat the oven to 50–60°C/120–140°F or if you have a gas oven as low as you can set it. (Beware though! If it is higher than 60°C the tomatoes will cook rather than dry).

2. Cut the tomatoes in half, place on a baking tray and sprinkle with salt, pepper, thyme and 1 tablespoon of olive oil.

3. Put into the oven and leave for about 7 hours, or overnight, to dry.

4. Transfer to a kilner jar and cover with olive oil, the sliced garlic and the thyme.

5. These will keep in the fridge for weeks.

TIPS

o You can use really cheap and tasteless tomatoes and they will still taste great when done. Good tomatoes will taste divine.

o The trick to these is to get the balance of time and heat right. If your oven is too low they will retain too much moisture in them and will not keep well (although they will taste plump and fine). If the oven is too hot, they will be partially cooked – again delicious, but not what we are after. You might need to experiment with a couple of batches before you work out what is best for your oven.

o A convection setting in the oven works best, as it takes out the moisture much more effectively.

Opposite: 'Sun-dried' Tomatoes before and after drying

LEON STRATEGY SALAMI

It takes a bit of time and preparation, but there is something life-changing about biting into a slice of your own salami.

Makes: 6–8 salamis
Preparation time: Quite a while (leave a lazy afternoon)
Curing time: 4 weeks–3 months
✓ WF DF GF

Equipment needed:
– a mincer with sausage filler attachment
– butcher's string

2 long **ox runners**, soaked overnight
2 teaspoons **fennel seeds**
1 clove of **garlic**
1.5kg **pork shoulder**
500g **pork fat** (ask your butcher for back fat)
2 teaspoons **black peppercorns**
salt – 2% of the weight of the meat + fat
400ml **spicy red wine** (e.g. Shiraz or Rioja)
a ready-made **salami** or **acidophilus** (you can buy this from the chemist – see step 8)

1. Snip the string on the ox runners and soak them overnight in a large quantity of cold water. Put each end up to the tap and rinse through with cold water. Put into a fresh bowl of cold water.

2. Dry roast the fennel in a pan. Peel the garlic and crush finely. Coarsely mince the pork shoulder. Chop the pork fat into little squares (like the ones you get in a salami).

3. Put all the ingredients except for the wine into a bowl and mix thoroughly (keeping the peppercorns whole). Make sure you weigh your salt carefully. Too much and it will be too salty, too little and the salami may go rotten.

4. Add the wine to the bowl gradually and mix it into the meat until it is absorbed.

5. Right, this is the fun bit. Fill your sausage filler. Stick two fingers into the end of an ox runner and dip it under the water. Now slide the whole runner on to the end of your sausage filler.

6. Squeeze out a little of the mix to make sure there is no air in the runner. Fold over the runner and tie it with a single knot, then flip over the loose end and tie it again. Fill the runner carefully, making it as tight and air-free as possible without the runner tearing (on your first attempt you will probably leave it a bit loose – don't worry, it will just turn out a little knobbly).

7. When you have a sausage at a length you like (20–30cm is a good size), tie it off again with a single knot, then flip it over and tie a double knot. Leave enough loose string to hang the salami. Continue until you are out of mix.

8. Hang the salamis in a cool airy place (a shed is perfect). Rub the skins with a cloth soaked in vinegar. At this point they will look hopelessly slippery and you will not believe that it will work. Rub on the whitened skin of an existing salami to the skin of your salamis to transfer some mould.

9. Wait between 4 and 12 weeks, depending on the climate and how hard you like your salami (you can tell how they are coming along by squeezing them).

Every year we take a few days away from Leon, to think about our strategy for the coming months. When the work is done we have some kind of feast, which usually involves butchering one of my step-mother's pigs and turning it into all manner of products – including this salami. *Henry*

SMOKING

There is a man who lives near to Henry in Hackney who smokes his own salmon in his garden. It is sublime. But it took him about 30 trial salmon to get it that way. The first drafts were salty and inedible. Unless you are willing to invest the time and the cash, smoking is one of those preserving techniques best left to the professionals. However, the organic-farmed bought stuff is sustainable, cheap and can be very good. There is a lot that you can do with it.

Our 6 favourite quick things to do with smoked salmon

1. **Put it on tagliatelle.** Heat some peas in double cream. Pepper it well (you shouldn't need salt). Drop in chunks of smoked salmon just before putting it on the pasta. Squeeze a bit of fresh lemon juice on top.

2. **Make a salad.** Peel and seed a cucumber, then chop it. Mix it with some cooked broad beans (pop them out of their greyish jackets if you have the patience). Add some chopped mint, lemon juice, olive oil and chunks of smoked salmon. Season.

3. **Drop it onto scrambled egg or into an omelette.** It's just very good.

4. **Make fake gravadlax:** Blitz the following ingredients and drizzle them on top: 1 tablespoon of Dijon mustard, 6 tablespoons of double cream, 1 tablespoon of honey, a large handful of dill, 1 tablespoon of white wine vinegar, salt and pepper to taste.

5. **Serve it as a smart starter with beetroot and horseradish:** Boil a couple of whole beetroots until soft, and peel them when cool (or buy them ready-cooked, whole). Chop the beetroot into 1cm cubes, chuck them into a bowl and drizzle with a tablespoon of balsamic vinegar and a teaspoon of olive oil. Season with salt and pepper and scatter over some chopped parsley. Lay the smoked salmon on a plate and dot it with the beetroot and shop-bought creamed horseradish.

6. **Use it to create a cheat's Ceviche.** If you can't get hold of good raw fish, you can make the ceviche recipe on page 148 with smoked salmon, only do not use the olive oil and be very liberal with the lemon juice to counteract the richness of the salmon.

FREEZING

Until recently, freezing was only a preservation option for the rich and for glacier dwellers. First trialled in Mesopotamia 4,000 years ago, ice houses were perfected by the Victorians to store their precious ice creams.

There are many things that can be made in advance and frozen – we normally have an assortment of stocks, soups and stews in our freezers (see page 12). The ultimate freezer treat, however, has to be ice cream. Making home-made ice cream is much simpler than most people think.

You will need some kind of ice cream machine to proceed beyond this point.

> If you do not have an ice cream maker all you need is a good timer and a whisk.
>
> 1. After you have made your ice cream mixture, transfer it into a plastic container or bowl, preferably with a lid.
> 2. Place it in the freezer for a couple of hours, or until it starts to solidify around the edges.
> 3. Remove it from the freezer and beat it thoroughly with a hand whisk or electric beater.
> 4. Return it to the freezer for a further two hours, and then repeat the beating process. Do this a few more times until the ice cream is set.
> 5. Don't forget to remove it from the freezer well in advance so that you can scoop it out easily.

VANILLA ICE CREAM

This is the base for almost all ice creams. Once you have mastered it, you can experiment by adding fruit, rum and raisins, salted caramel, you name it…

Makes: 900ml
Preparation time: 20 minutes
+ freezing time
WF GF

5 **egg yolks**
1 **vanilla pod**
500ml **double cream**
100ml **milk**
180g **caster sugar**
sea salt

1. Make sure the eggs are at room temperature. You will only be using the yolks for this recipe.

2. Halve the vanilla pod lengthways and put it into a pan with the cream, milk and sugar. Bring to the boil, stirring to make sure the sugar dissolves. Allow to stand for 5 minutes.

3. Meanwhile put the egg yolks into a blender and blend for 5 minutes, or until they go creamy. Add a small pinch of salt.

4. Bring the cream back to the boil and pour it slowly on to the eggs, blending as you go. Assuming that the cream is good and hot and the eggs not too cold, you should be left with great not-too-thick custard. (If you want to make it thicker heat it gently on the hob, but you shouldn't need to.)

5. Let it cool to room temperature, then pour it through a sieve into an ice cream machine and freeze. It will be best within 4 days (even in the freezer).

Back: Deep Chocolate Ice Cream; Front: Vanilla Ice Cream & Raspberry Ripple

DEEP CHOCOLATE ICE CREAM

We have experimented for some time to get a deep dark chocolate ice cream. The breakthrough came when we added cocoa powder – traditionally looked down on. It adds real depth of flavour and improves the texture.

Makes: 900ml
Preparation time: 20 minutes
+ freezing time
WF GF V

5 **egg yolks**
120ml **milk**
30ml **double cream**
90g **chocolate** (70% cocoa solids)
130g **caster sugar**
30g **cocoa**

1. Make sure the eggs are at room temperature. You will only be using the yolks for this recipe.

2. Bring the milk and cream to the boil. Add the chocolate and allow to melt.

3. Put the egg yolks into a bowl, add the sugar and cocoa and beat well. Whisk in a little of the hot cream/milk mix, then put everything into a pan and return it to the stove. Heat gently, stirring well, for 10 minutes. It will bubble – don't worry.

4. Pour through a sieve and leave to cool.

5. Freeze in an ice cream machine. Best eaten within 4 days.

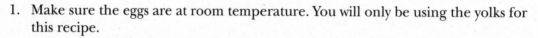

TIPS

○ Make some hazelnut cracknell (see page 194) and add it to the machine when it is a little stiff but still not frozen.

RASPBERRY RIPPLE

You can leave out the vodka if you are making this for children, but it really lifts the flavour of the raspberries (and the spirits).

Makes: 900ml
Preparation time: 20 minutes
WF GF V

vanilla ice cream (see page 273)
1 punnet of **raspberries**
4 level tablespoons **icing sugar**
2 tablespoons **vodka**

1. Make the vanilla ice cream.

2. Put the raspberries, icing sugar and vodka into a blender and blitz to a thickish purée.

3. Before the ice cream is fully frozen (but once it is pretty stiff), stir through the raspberries in thick seams. Continue to freeze.

SACHA'S CANJA

A last word. We couldn't find a proper space for this recipe but we love it so we put it here. A fab dish for when you are feeling lousy.

Feeds: 4
Preparation time: 10 minutes
Cooking time: 15 minutes
♥ ✓ WF GF

1 **onion**
200g **chicken thighs**
olive oil
200g **basmati rice**
900ml **chicken stock**
2 tablespoons **crème fraîche** or **double cream**
sea salt and **freshly ground black pepper**

1. Slice the onions and cut the chicken roughly into pieces. Heat a little oil in a casserole or deep saucepan and sauté the onions until softened, then add the chicken and cook until browned a little. Add the rice and cook for 1 minute.

2. Add the chicken stock to the pan and cook for 10 minutes, or until the rice is tender.

3. Add the crème fraîche or cream and season with salt and pepper.

TIPS

○ You can use left-over chicken from a roast – just add it towards the end of the cooking time.

○ Add more stock if you want it to be more of a soup.

○ Serve with Parmesan shavings and a drizzle of olive oil, or with a spot of harissa (pictured).

○ Serve with crusty bread and a green salad.

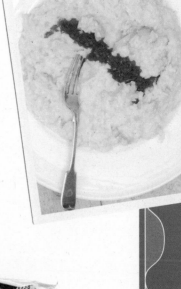

Sacha (far right) with the family, 1950

Sacha – my wife Katie's aunt – used to live in Brazil, and this is an adaptation of one of her recipes. Great for when you are feeling shocking, or just as an easy supper.
John

FRIENDS & FAMILY RECIPES

BONUS FEATURES

Cocktails

Cocktails are naughty, which is what makes them so nice. A dream in a glass; a beach welcome; a Christmas sing-song with Dean Martin. Possibilities. Maybe even probabilities.

Tom is the king of the silver shaker at Leon. Strictly speaking, his job is to oversee the restaurant managers, but old habits die hard: he was a bartender before joining Leon, and at all our parties you'll find him back in Tom Cruise mode, juggling bottles of arcane spirits with his former colleague and conspirator, Giles. By the end of the evening he'll be on the dance floor reaping the rewards of his making.

These are Tom's top six tipples. Proceed with care. Over to you Tom…

CHRISTMAS COCKTAIL

I first drank this in a smart Soho bar and realized immediately that my mum would love it. I made it last Christmas for the family. Mum did love it, Dad drank far too much of it. Substitute berry cordial for Campari and use soda water instead of prosecco, and the kids can join in, too.

Feeds: 6

120ml **Campari**
60ml **lemon juice**
120ml **clementine juice**
70ml **sugar syrup** (see below)
420ml **prosecco**
orange zest, for garnish

Sugar syrup: Put equal parts caster sugar and tap water (200g and 200ml) into a small jug, stir and leave to stand (stirring occasionally) until the sugar dissolves. Should take about 20 minutes.

1. In a cocktail shaker combine the Campari, lemon juice, clementine juice and sugar syrup.

2. Add ice and shake.

3. Strain the mixture equally into 6 champagne glasses and top with prosecco. Garnish with a twist of orange zest.

HOT HALLOWE'EN PUNCH

It was Hallowe'en 2009, and Giles and I were at a party at the 'Lady Castle' in Peckham (a big house full of beautiful single girls). Giles had the idea of making a hot punch – it was freezing outside. We used various bits and bobs that he found in the kitchen and came up with this. The party went with a swing, and this concoction is now a must every Hallowe'en.

Feeds: about 20

400ml **brandy**
1.5 litres **West Country dry cide**r
10 tablespoons **sugar**
300ml **lemon juice**
10 dashes of **Angostura bitters**
2–3 **cinnamon sticks**
5–6 **cloves**
lemon zest for garnish

1. Pour all the ingredients except the lemon zest into a large pan and bring to a slow simmer.

2. Ladle into beakers and garnish with a twist of lemon zest.

SOUL FRUIT CUP

Giles now runs his own company called Soul Shakers, travelling the world making cocktails at some of the best parties in the world (lucky boy). He put together a cocktail bar at Henley for the Regatta and served his version of Pimm's. Perfect to sip on a hot summer's day, while others work up a sweat.

Feeds: 6

100ml **gin**
75ml **Campari**
100ml **sweet vermouth**
150ml **pink grapefruit juice**
juice of 2 **lemons**
6–8 slices of **cucumber**
lemonade (homemade or bottled)
strawberries and **mint** for garnish
 – optional

1. Pour the alcohol, grapefruit juice and lemon juice into a jug.

2. Add the cucumber and lemonade and stir.

3. Pour into iced glasses and garnish with strawberries and/or mint if you like.

LEON SUMMER PUNCH

Think summer, all your best friends, your back garden, a balmy evening and an England World Cup victory.

Feeds: 6

16 **strawberries**
2 **pears** (nice and ripe)
150ml **sugar syrup** (see page 278)
150ml **vodka**
120ml **lemon juice**
bottle of prosecco

1. Blend the strawberries and pears to make a simple purée, adding the sugar syrup to sweeten.

2. Put the purée into a jug and mix in the vodka and lemon juice.

3. Top with prosecco and stir. Pour into champagne flutes and toast the Queen.

VODKA ESPRESSO

This drink has been a favourite of the London bar scene since the mid-nineties. Rumour has it that its birthplace was the Pharmacy – Damien Hirst's now defunct joint in Notting Hill. An experienced barman can tell how many of these caffeine-loaded cocktails a customer has had from the twitching in the arm or the judder of the head. Be warned: after three it is almost impossible to sit down.

Feeds: 1

40ml **vodka**
20ml **Kahlua**
35ml **espresso**
caster sugar
coffee beans for garnish
 – optional

1. In a cocktail shaker combine the vodka, Kahlua, espresso and a dash of sugar (it's up to you how sweet you like it). Pack it full of ice and shake it really hard for about 10 seconds: you want a nice froth on top, so shake it good.

2. Pour into a martini glass or champagne flute and garnish with 3 coffee beans if you have them.

3. This recipe is for one cocktail. You can probably fit two in one shaker, but any more than that and you'll lose the lovely crème on top.

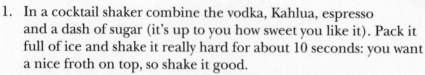

KAMOMILLA FIZZ

This is a slightly more taxing drink, for those of you who fancy yourselves as cocktail connoisseurs. I invented it for the International Finlandia Vodka Cup in 2006. It won the best long drink and we served bucketloads at the Big Chill the same year. The camomile and cucumber work beautifully together, and it's a great long summer drink. You can substitute the vodka with gin, which also works really well (it's known as a 10cc).

Feeds: 1

3 slices of **cucumber** (about the thickness of a pound coin)
½ a **lemon**, cut into 4 wedges
25ml **camomile tea syrup** (see below)
40ml **vodka**
ice
sparkling water or **soda water**

In a cocktail shaker, muddle the cucumber and 3 of the lemon wedges with 25ml of camomile tea syrup. Muddle it quite hard to work the juice and oil out of the lemon. Add the vodka and ice and shake for a good 10 seconds. Strain into an ice-filled highball glass. Top with sparkling water or soda. Garnish with the remaining lemon wedge. Kippis!

Camomile tea syrup: Make a strong brew of camomile tea – about 3 teabags in 200ml of hot water. Leave it to stand for 5 minutes. Remove the teabags and add 200g of caster sugar, then stir until the sugar has dissolved and leave to cool.

Giles in Key West, 1982

FRIENDS & FAMILY RECIPES

Tom and his brother Patrick doing AC/DC, Sheffield, 1988

BEHIND THE SCENES at a Leon party...

FROM FARMS WE TRUST

Since Leon opened in July 2004 we have relied heavily on the wisdom and experience of the people who rear our meat. Farming in the UK is hard work for little reward, and three people in particular have gone out of their way to support us as we've grown.

Andy Maunder

Andy Maunder's hands were black from picking walnuts when we first met him. We liked him immediately. Since that day he has been in charge of making our chickens happy at his farm in Devon.

Dealing with Leon is wonderful; proper people buying proper chicken. When buying chicken they want a great tasting product but, just as important they want a sustainable, welfare-friendly, rural-job-creating, wildlife-promoting, natural, as it used to taste, chicken. 'Proper job' as we say in the West Country. *Andy*

Basil and Richard

Basil and Richard, a father and son team also from Devon, make terrific sausages and the best additive-free bacon we have ever tasted.

Andy, Basil and Richard. Thank you.

Leon is an exciting venture for us here at Devon Rose. We make Leon bacon and sausages from free range pork raised here on the unique Jurassic pasture land on the South Devon coast, mixed with our own blend of herbs and spices. We feel that we share their philosophy and love of great food. For Leon, we use a mixture of rare, traditional and modern breeds all noted for purity, taste and eating quality.

Basil (left) and son Richard (middle)

SUSTAINABILITY

Henry recently helped to set up the Sustainable Restaurant Association: a not-for-profit organization that helps restaurants to do business with a clean conscience. There are all sorts of things that restaurateurs can do to tread more lightly on the earth, from watching our water usage to using fish from sustainable stocks. You can do the same at home by following a few simple principles.

Eat much less meat and dairy

Rearing animals to turn into meat or produce milk consumes profligate quantities of water, land and energy. If we all ate a completely vegetarian diet for two days a week, the CO_2 saved would be equivalent to building ten nuclear power stations. Switching to a more vegetable-based diet, with meat, fish and dairy as an occasional side dish rather than the main event, has the added advantage of saving you money and making you feel – and look – a million dollars.

Eat sustainable fish

We are constantly being told to eat more fish, yet global fish stocks are in serious peril. Working out which of our scaly friends you can safely tuck into can seem impossibly complicated, but www.fishonline.org is a great resource.

Eat more seasonally

This becomes easier to do if you order your vegetables in a weekly seasonal box or you have a good greengrocer. (Otherwise it requires a keen eye and disciplined hand at the supermarket.)

Shop much more at markets and local shops

This was tricky ten years ago, but since then Britain has seen a miraculous explosion in food markets. The sellers are more likely to know the provenance of their food (and, at farmers' markets, to have produced it themselves). As an added bonus, the food tends to be less shrouded in unnecessary packaging.

Compost your peelings

If your garden isn't big enough for a compost heap, get a wormery. Worms are arguably easier to manage, and certainly more fun (especially for terrorizing visiting children). They'll eat almost anything, apart from onions, garlic, citrus fruits, spicy food, meat and fish and turn it into a lovely rich juice which can then be sprinkled on to your plants as fertilizer. Failing that, most councils will now collect domestic food waste to put on their own giant municipal compost heaps or even get turned into fertilizer and energy through anaerobic digestion. Anything is better than sending it to landfill.

RECIPES FROM LEON MANAGERS

The managers at Leon are some of the hardest-working, most generous and enthusiastic people you are ever likely to meet.

They are also damn fine cooks, and extremely competitive, as we discovered at a cook-off in Henry's kitchen to get their recipes into this book.

These are the winners.

ESMARELDA'S MELK KOS (MILK PUDDING)

Feeds: 8
Preparation time: 5 minutes
Cooking time: 15 minutes

 ᵛ

2 tablespoons **flour**
2 tablespoons **cornflour**
½ cup **sugar**
pinch of **salt**
3 **eggs**
1 **vanilla pod**
2 litres **milk**
125g **butter**
ground cinnamon for dusting

Esmarelda and her son James, 1998

RECIPE TESTED BY. JAMES

1. In a large bowl mix together the flour, cornflour, sugar, salt and eggs.

2. Cut the vanilla pod open and place in a large thick-bottomed pan with the milk and butter.

3. Gently bring the milk mixture to the boil. As soon as the milk is boiling, take it off the heat, remove the vanilla pod and add the flour and egg mixture slowly while stirring. The mixture will start thickening straight away.

4. Place the pan back on a low heat, and simmer for about 5 minutes, still stirring.

5. Remove from the heat, divide between bowls and sprinkle the ground cinnamon on top. Eat while warm!

 TIPS

o You can use this wonderful milk pudding to make a tart. Simply make a basic shortcrust pastry, line a tart case, fill it with the milk pudding, and bake in the oven for 10 minutes at 180°C/350°F/gas mark 4. Scatter the cinnamon on top.

FRIENDS & FAMILY RECIPES

THEO'S CHICKPEA CURRY

Theo is our manager Tom's girlfriend. She makes this with either tinned chickpeas (cheap) or dried chickpeas (ridiculously cheap).

Feeds: 4
Preparation time: 10 minutes
Cooking time: about 1 hour
♥ ✓ WF DF GF V

1 **onion**
5 cloves of **garlic**
2 **red chillies**
an 8cm piece of **fresh ginger**
2 tablespoons **oil**
1 teaspoon **turmeric**
½ teaspoon **ground cumin**
1½ teaspoon **ground coriander**
1 teaspoon **garam masala**
3 x 400g tins of **chickpeas**
1 x 400g tin of **chopped tomatoes**
2 handfuls of **fresh coriander**
sea salt and **freshly ground black pepper**

1. Peel and finely chop the onion, garlic and chillies. Peel then grate the ginger on the fine edge of your grater.

2. Heat the oil in a thick-bottomed pan and fry the onion on a medium heat, stirring often. Add the garlic, chillies and ginger and fry for 2 minutes.

3. Add the spices and fry for a further 5 minutes. You might find that it all balls up and sticks to the pan, in which case add a bit more oil.

4. Drain the chickpeas and add to the pan, stirring to coat them well in the spices. Then add the tinned tomatoes. The curry should be quite liquidy.

5. Simmer gently for 45 minutes to an hour, until the flavours come together and the spices don't taste bitter. Stir occasionally. If it dries up, add a bit of stock (which I make with Marigold bouillon powder – the tastiest).

6. Chop the coriander and add to the pan. Season with salt and pepper.

TIPS

o Add spinach to the curry if you like. Put it in with the coriander, salt and pepper, and it will wilt down very quickly.

o You can vary the flavours by adding cardamom seeds and fenugreek, or dry-roasted coriander and cumin seeds, crushed in a pestle and mortar.

Tom at Docklow Manor, 1985

OT'S HOT CHEESE: EGYPTIAN GIBNA

Feeds: 4
Preparation time: 5 minutes
Cooking time: 0 minutes
✓ WF GF V

200g **gibna beyda** or **Greek feta cheese**
2 tablespoons **tahini**
2 tablespoons **olive oil**
½ teaspoon **chilli powder**
a handful of chopped **fresh mint**
freshly ground black pepper

1. Cut the gibna beyda or feta cheese into cubes and put into a large bowl.

2. Add the tahini, olive oil, chilli powder, mint and pepper, and stir thoroughly.

3. Eat it on warmed flat bread with cold meat and salad, or serve it with chopped mangoes.

 TIPS

○ Add more chilli powder if you can handle the heat.

BY AIRMAIL
PAR AVION

I was in the middle of nowhere in Egypt and found myself invited for lunch by a shoe polisher and his wife. She gave me instructions on how to make this lovely spicy dish before I headed off to the pyramids... *Otoa*

Ot and her dad's favourite mixtape, Japan, 1984

RECIPE TESTED BY ELLA & LILY

RECIPE TESTED BY MAGNUS

FRIENDS & FAMILY RECIPES

ROY'S FIRE CRACKER SOUP

Feeds: 4
Preparation time: 10 minutes
Cooking time: 20 minutes
♥ ✓ WF DF GF V

3 **onions**
1 clove of **garlic**
1 **carrot**
a small piece of **fresh ginger**
1 stick of **celery**
1 tablespoon **vegetable oil**
1 litre **vegetable stock**, fresh or made with 2 stock cubes
2 x 400g tins of **chopped tomatoes**
2 **tomatoes**
a few **fresh basil leaves**
tomato purée
½ teaspoon **mustard powder**
sea salt and **freshly ground pepper**

1. Peel and finely chop the onions and garlic. Dice the carrot, celery and ginger.

2. Heat a small amount of oil in a saucepan and add the onions, garlic, celery, carrot and ginger.

3. Add the stock and cook until the vegetables are soft.

4. When cooked, put everything into a blender or food processor, adding the tinned and fresh tomatoes and the basil leaves. Blitz and return the mixture to the pan.

5. Add a generous squirt of tomato purée, stir in the mustard powder and season with salt and pepper.

TIPS
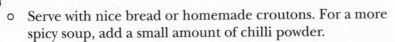

○ Serve with nice bread or homemade croutons. For a more spicy soup, add a small amount of chilli powder.

○ Using too many fresh tomatoes can make the soup too sweet.

With the exception of Christmas, bonfire night has become the only other regular family gathering in the Bowerman household. Every year, our family comes together in my parent's back garden to watch the catherine wheels, fountains and rockets, and we oversee this classic display with mulled wine and – in the words of my father Roy – his 'fast, famous and furious firework night soup'. *Ursula*

Ursula's brother Morton, dad Roy and mother Jennie

FRIENDS & FAMILY
RECIPES

SCREAM *IF YOU WANT TO GO* FASTER

LEON

NATURALLY FAST FOOD

THE BIG CHILL

Last summer Leon packed its tent, unwrapped its glowsticks and headed to Herefordshire for the Big Chill festival.

As well as manning a stall near the main stage, we cooked the cakes for a tea party in Eastnor Castle at which Mr Scruff served tea and Alice Russell sang.

We also served our first ever customers dressed as zombies.

PIERRE'S BIG CHILL SALAD

The highlight of the festival, at least for some of us, was a barbecue that we held backstage for Leon regulars. Henry cooked great chunks of lamb, black pudding, spatchcocked chickens and Porterhouse steaks. But the best thing was the enormous salad thrown together at the last minute by our friend Pierre.

Feeds: 4
Preparation time: 5 minutes
Cooking time: 0 minutes
♥ ✓ WF DF GF V

4 ripe **tomatoes**
a tin of **cooked sweet peppers**
2 ripe **avocados**
a large handful of **fresh flat-leaf parsley**
juice of 1 **lemon**
a great glug of **olive oil** – poured from a height
a large head of **cos lettuce**
sea salt and **freshly ground black pepper**

1. Quarter the tomatoes. Chop the peppers, keeping the juice from the tin. Roughly chop the avocados and parsley. One reason this salad was so good was because of the way it was tossed. Put all the ingredients except the lettuce into a bowl and season well. Toss them energetically. Get your hands in there, up to the elbows if necessary. The avocado should begin to break up a little. Toss it again.

2. Sit in the sun for a while. At the last moment chop the lettuce and add to the salad. Check the seasoning again. Serve.

Pictures opposite by Rob Orchard and Steve Razzetti

DRAWERS OF WISHES

We have a chest in the Leon at Ludgate Circus with many drawers. No one knows quite how it started, but over the years it has filled up with the wishes of people who eat with us.

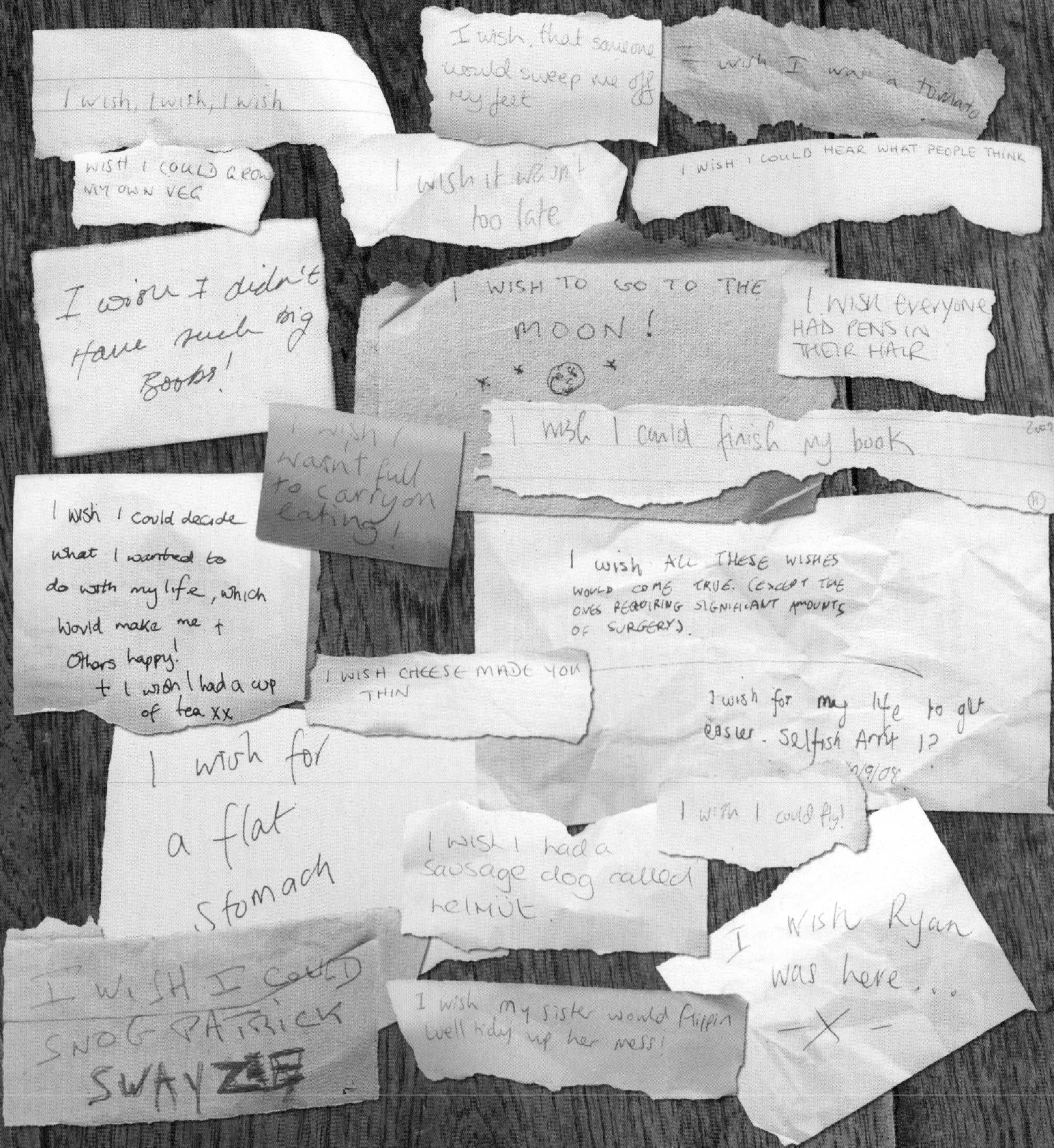

I wish, I wish, I wish

I wish, that someone would sweep me off my feet

I wish I was a tomato

WISH I COULD GROW MY OWN VEG

I wish it wasn't too late

I WISH I COULD HEAR WHAT PEOPLE THINK

I wish I didn't have such big Boobs!

I WISH TO GO TO THE MOON!

I WISH EVERYONE HAD PENS IN THEIR HAIR

I wish I wasn't full to carry on eating!

I wish I could finish my book   2009

I wish I could decide what I wanted to do with my life, which would make me + Others happy! + I wish I had a cup of tea xx

I WISH ALL THESE WISHES WOULD COME TRUE. (EXCEPT THE ONES REQUIRING SIGNIFICANT AMOUNTS OF SURGERY).

I WISH CHEESE MADE YOU THIN

I wish for my life to get easier. Selfish Arrh! ? 2/9/08

I wish for a flat stomach

I WISH I had a sausage dog called helmut.

I wish I could fly!

I WISH I COULD SNOG PATRICK SWAYZE

I wish my sister would flippin well tidy up her mess!

I wish Ryan was here... -X-

LONDON W1F 7JE
LEON.
35-36 Gt. MARLBOROUGH St.
Fair Trade & Organic
NOME DEL PASSEGGERO _____
BAGAGLIAIO

LEON
Pure Flavour

FRESH FISH
from sustainable shoals
DOLPHIN FRIENDLY

1 2 3 4 5 6 7 8 9 10 11 12 S
THE LEON GOBI

SUPERFOOD SALAD
LEON ORIGINAL

LEON-HOTEL
CASABLANCA

LEON
15 GREAT MARLBOROUGH STREET · LONDON · W1F 7JE   T: 020 7432 5280

LEON
Full of Sun
35 GT. MARLBOROUGH ST.
LONDON

LEON
OUR FISH IS FROM SUSTAINABLE SHOALS OR FARMED ORGANICALLY

LEON   LDN.

I wish to fall in love!
I WISH I WAS A POLAR BEAR
I WISH MY GRANDMA WAS HERE.
I wish I was sane
I WISH I WAS WRITING THE MOST BEAUTIFUL BOOK EVER UPON AN ITALIAN TERRACE WITH AN ENDLESS SUPPLY OF PASTA, CHAMPAGNE AND SUNDRESSES
I WISH MY JOB DIDN'T SUCK.
I wish Greg would move to London.
I wish I knew what this drawer was for

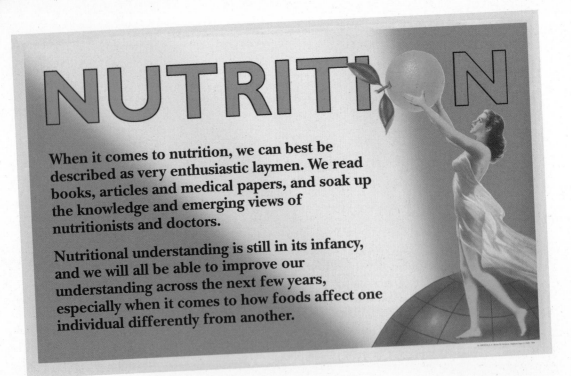

NUTRITION

When it comes to nutrition, we can best be described as very enthusiastic laymen. We read books, articles and medical papers, and soak up the knowledge and emerging views of nutritionists and doctors.

Nutritional understanding is still in its infancy, and we will all be able to improve our understanding across the next few years, especially when it comes to how foods affect one individual differently from another.

Here, we'd like to explain the significance behind the icons we use and how these principles might be useful to you as you shop and eat more generally.

✓ We use the ✓ symbol to denote dishes that have a low 'Glycemic Load' or GL. This is a concept that has become much better understood in the past five years. It is slightly different from the more famous Glycemic Index (GI), which measures the sugariness of the carbohydrate within each food, on a scale relative to glucose (which ranks at 100). On the GI all foods with a score above 50 are seen as bad news, even though some – a carrot, say – might contain only a small amount of the offending carbohydrate.

The Glycemic Load, by contrast, measures the effect of the whole food (i.e. the whole carrot), not just the sugary element. This means that carrots, which score badly on the Glycemic Index, score well on GL because they contain very little carbohydrate. What matters – in terms of keeping you healthy – is the extent to which a food raises your blood sugar levels as it is digested, promoting the build-up of fat. We give any dish with a GL of under 10 a ✓.

♥ These dishes have less than 1.5% saturated fat. Most people need to eat more oily fats such as olive oil, fishy fats, the fats found in vegetables such as avocado, in seeds and nuts, and even goose fat. These are now recognized as essential to health and even weight-loss. (There are a very few people who actually need to eat more hard, saturated fats.) None of our food has modified fats such as trans fats.

W F For a number of reasons, wheat has become a problem for many people. Modern wheat is very different from traditional 'old' grains such as buckwheat, millet, spelt and kamut. Over the centuries it has been bred to be easier to harvest and higher-yielding. Along the way, the average gluten content of wheat has soared from 2% to 50%, perhaps accounting for the increase in wheat intolerance. There is also evidence that the protein in wheat germ is causing health issues for many people.

D F All mammals, including man, need milk in infancy. But as adults many of us lose the enzymes needed to digest milk and other dairy products, leading to digestive problems. Thus the DF icon.

G F Coeliac disease is the most extreme manifestation of gluten intolerance. But research suggests that all of us would be healthier if we cut down on gluten – the protein that gives many starches their stickiness. It exists in wheat, rye, barley and other related grains – but not in any of these dishes.

V Vegetarian. Because we should all be eating more veg.

Indulgence. We believe in letting our hair down occasionally. These dishes – to be enjoyed on special occasions – will invigorate the spirit.

So what general advice can one give? Most of us thrive best on moderate portions of naturally produced food, predominantly vegetables, with plenty of the foods that we used to scavenge for: seeds, berries, nuts. And with side helpings of meat. As Michael Pollan says in his excellent *In Defense of Food*: 'Eat food. Not too much. Mostly plants.'

We've spoken to a lot of people along the way to deepen our understanding of nutrition and among those who we'd like to thank are Yvonne Bishop-Weston and Carole Symons who have been particularly helpful.

Henry and Liza, southern Spain, August 1977

INDEX

INDEX

INDEX

INDEX

INDEX

Charlie Bigham • Nicola Williams • Guy McLaren • Helen Vaughan • Helen Cruise • Laura Schofield • Jamie Gorman • Monica Peswani • Lloyd Hughes • Tom Bell • Mark Latham • Kenny McColl • Martin Bull • Russell Loveland • David Atcherley-Symes • Camille Waxer • Henry Togna • Paul Wakefield • Ben Kilshaw • Nigel Mason • Andy Maunder • Craig & Clare Barton • Clare Mugglestone • Carly Stevenson • Birgit Gunz • Emma & Matt Goss-Custard • Simon Pritchard • Derek Aston • Guy Lingard • Gary Ashcroft • Kevin Hayler • Nick Wood • Caroline Babington • Monica Wolff • David Kaye • Martin Sansom • Mary Purnell • Alex Maynard

Skye Gygnell for inspiring a whole new breed of Leon wrap

Nick Stratton for showing people how great a human being can be

Sandra whose initial Leon designs live on

Thank you to Katie 'the wife' Derham for constant sunshine, encouragement and ideas

To all of you who have eaten with us & allowed us to realize the first steps of our dreams

JoJo for her gardening wisdom

Bambi Sloane for riding the roller coaster and still managing to design whilst on it – you channel the spirit of a thousand artists

Richard Reed for being my life-twin and for the foot thing (although I can never be Sifu Sifu Jones)

Vivian Imerman for being the Godfather

Simon, Benny, James, Tom, Rich, Agnieszka, and Steve for keeping the Leon show on the road

Fred for his infectious enthusiasm

Jane at the Riverford Farm Field Kitchen for helping me see vegetables in a new light

Xander, Adam, Dave, Becca, Lloyd, James, Ian, Susana, Jonathan, Michele, & Belinda for believing in Leon from the start

Anita for doing away with sleep to get this book out of the door (almost) on time

Annie Lee for copy editing

Allegra for everything she did to get us up and running

THANK YOU

Steph Morison for being a brilliant human being

Natasha and Eleanor for fierce loyalty. And for being brilliant, loving daughters.

Alice Denford for bringing new dimensions.

Claire for the cakes

David Griffiths for advertently and inadvertently giving me everything I have had since the start

Mattma, Maddie and Cy for props, love & patience

Marc Rogers • Sophie Douglas • Roger Gascoigne • Rick Hudson • Tony Bamford-Mumby • Jack Sharkey • Chris Rouine • Adrian Eade • Andy Oldham • Vic Madhu Simon Watkins • Anne Philippe • Leticia Godet • Peter Wakeling • Fabio Di Palma • Dan Taylor • Yvette Doughty • Nick Wesley • Abigail Lawley • Jethro McCarthy Jon Horsfield • Cara Coan • Alecia Mitchell • Ian Carpenter • Rod Adlington • James Fincham • The Big Chill tent construction gang • Andy Kellar • Gemma Alashe

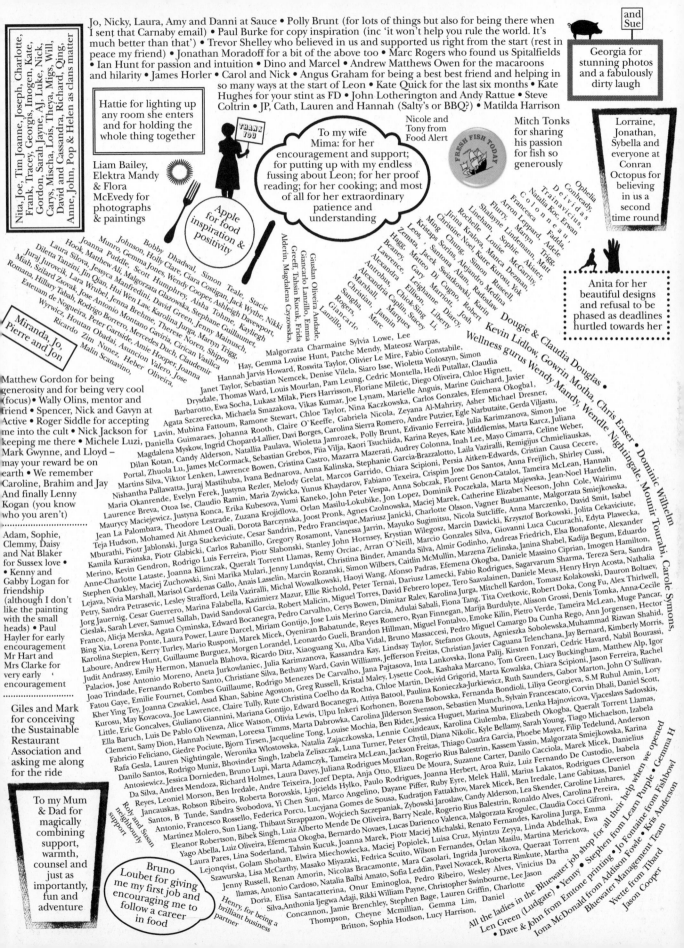

Jo, Nicky, Laura, Amy and Danni at Sauce • Polly Brunt (for lots of things but also for being there when I sent that Carnaby email) • Paul Burke for copy inspiration (inc 'it won't help you rule the world. It's much better than that') • Trevor Shelley who believed in us and supported us right from the start (rest in peace my friend) • Jonathan Moradoff for a bit of the above too • Marc Rogers who found us Spitalfields • Ian Hunt for passion and intuition • Dino and Marcel • Andrew Matthews Owen for the macaroons and hilarity • James Horler • Carol and Nick • Angus Graham for being a best best friend and helping in so many ways at the start of Leon • Kate Quick for the last six months • Kate Hughes for your stint as FD • John Lotherington and Andy Rattue • Steve Coltrin • JP, Cath, Lauren and Hannah (Salty's or BBQ?) • Matilda Harrison

and Sue

Georgia for stunning photos and a fabulously dirty laugh

Nita, Joe, Tim Joanne, Joseph, Charlotte, Frank, Tracey, Georgis, Imogen, Kate, Gordon, Sarah Jane, AJ, Luke, Nick, Carys, Mischa, Lois, Theya, Migs, Will, David and Cassandra, Richard, Qing, Anne, John, Pop & Helen as clans matter

Hattie for lighting up any room she enters and for holding the whole thing together

THANK YOU

Nicole and Tony from Food Alert

Mitch Tonks for sharing his passion for fish so generously

FRESH FISH TODAY

To my wife Mima: for her encouragement and support; for putting up with my endless fussing about Leon; for her proof reading; for her cooking; and most of all for her extraordinary patience and understanding

Lorraine, Jonathan, Sybella and everyone at Conran Octopus for believing in us a second time round

Liam Bailey, Elektra Mandy & Flora McEvedy for photographs & paintings

Apple for food inspiration & positivity

Ophelia Conheady, Deivida Trainavicius, Natalia Koc, Erwan Colonneu, Francesca Fadda, Arron Leppard, Adele Martyn, Trigg, Shalayne Lindemann, Matt Flurry, Akister, Rochelle Louise McCarthy, Jirina Kralova, Manca Dezman, Christine Noel, Katre Kurosti, Yok Ming Chung, Simon Russell, Kristaps Sorins, Alejandro Medina, Zemsta, Jacek Swiatkowski, Radoslaw Leos, Santona Alam, Gary Marriott, Robert Beaney, Matteo Di Cugno, Karin Lawrence, Leighanne Diarcy, Alexandra, Ellison, Josh, Antrobus, Chiok-Sing Li, Marshall, Caplin, Stacey Li, Christian, Marques Sangha, Jasmin Rogers, Giancarlo Marc Giancarlo Lanzillo, Giancarlo Lanzillo, Emma Greff, Tahsin Kucuk, Frida Alderin, Magdalena Czyzowska,

Giusian Oliveira Andade, Stacie Bobby Dhadwal, Simon Teale, Johnson, Holly Clare, Ciara Costigan, Jack Wythe, Nikki Joanna Puddle, Wendy Cooper, Ashleigh Davewport, Kayliegh Munro, Gemma Jones, Hook, Matthew Ali, Scott Humphrey, Aisha Tohme, Laura Silova, Jessyca Manfredini, Malgorzata Glazowska, Diletta Tanzini, Jin Qian, Hui Wen Law, David Green, Stephane Guillaumet, Juraj Jurovcik, Lara Wrubel, Jenna Brehme, Karolina Jurga, Martyn Trigg, Miah, Szilard Zsovak, Jose Antonio Montano Gaviria, Therese Noren, Shipon Romana, Hillary Tabah, Rodrigo Borrero, Mercedes Duch, Cirican Vasilica Esteuam de Nogueira, Peter Gartside, Amie Hooper, Claudemir Wyrwicz, Houtan Obadai, Asuncion Valero, Jose Ricardo Zim Nunez, Heber Oliveira, Malin Scanavino,

Malgorzata Charmaine Sylvia Lowe, Lee Hay, Gemma Louise Hunt, Patche Mendy, Mateosz Warpas, Hannah Jarvis Howard, Roswita Taylor, Olivier Le Mire, Fabio Constabile, Janet Taylor, Sebastian Nemcek, Denise Vilela, Siaro Isse, Wioletta Woloszyn, Simon Drysdale, Thomas Ward, Louis Mourlan, Pam Leung, Cedric Montella, Hedi Putallaz, Claudia Barbarotto, Ewa Socha, Lukasz Milak, Piers Harrisson, Floriane Miletic, Diego Oliveira, Chloe Hignett, Agata Szczerecka, Michaela Smazakova, Vikas Kumar, Joe Lynam, Marielle Anguis, Marine Guichard, Javier Lavin, Mubina Fattoum, Ramone Stewart, Chloe Taylor, Nina Kaczkowska, Zeyana Al-Mahrizy, Asher Michael Dresner, Daniella Guimaraes, Johanna Rooth, Claire O'Keeffe, Gabriela Nicola, Andre Putzier, Egle Narbutaite, Gerda Viljastu, Magdalena Myskow, Ingrid Chopard-Lallier, Davi Borges, Carolina Sierra Romero, Edivanio Ferreira, Julia Karimzanova, Simon Joe Dilan Kotan, Candy Alderson, Natallia Paulava, Wioletta Jamrozek, Polly Brunt, Kate Middlemiss, Marta Karcz, Juliana Portal, Zhuola Lu, James McCormack, Sebastian Grebos, Piia Vilja, Kaori Tsuchiida, Karina Reyes, Inah Lee, Mayo Cimarra, Celine Weber, Martins Silva, Viktor Lenken, Lawrence Bowen, Cristina Castro, Mazarra Mazerati, Audrey Colonna, Laila Vaziralli, Remigijus Chmieliauskas, Nishantha Pallawata, Juraj Mastihuba, Ivana Bednarova, Anna Kalinska, Stephanie Garcia-Brazzalotto, Cristian Causa Cecere, Maria Okanrende, Evelyn Ferek, Justyna Rezler, Melody Grelat, Marcos Garrido, Chiara Scipioni, Persia Aitken-Edwards, Shirley Cussi, Laurence Breva, Otoa Ise, Claudio Ramin, Maria Zywicka, Yunus Khaydarov, John Peter Vespa, Anna Sobczak, Florent Genon-Catalot, Tameira McLean, Hannah Maurycy Maciejewicz, Justyna Konca, Erika Kubesova, Zuzana Krojidlova, Orlan Masilu-Lokubike, Jon Lopez, Dominik Poczekala, Marta Majewska, Jean-Noel Hardelin, Jean La Palombara, Theodore Lestrade, Dorota Barczynska, Joost Pronk, Agnes Czolnowska, Maciej Marek, Catherine Elizabet Neeson, John Cole, Wairimu Mburathi, Piotr Jablonski, Jurga Stackeviciute, Cesar Sandrin, Pedro Francisque, Mariusz Janicki, Charlotte Olsson, Vagner Bustamante, Malgorzata Smiejkowska, Isabel Kamila Kurasinska, Piotr Glabicki, Carlos Rabanillo, Piotr Slabonski, Stanley John Hornsey, Krystian Wilegosz, Marcin Dawicki, Krzysztof Borkowski, Jolita Cekaviciute, Merino, Kevin Gendron, Rodrigo Luis Ferreira, Piotr Slabonski, Remy Orciac, Arran O'Neill, Marcio Gonzales Silva, Giovanni Luca Cucurachi, Edyta Plawecka, Anne-Charlotte Lataste, Joanna Klimczak, Queralt Torrent Llamas, Jenny Lundqvist, Christina Binder, Amanda Silva, Almir Godinho, Andreas Friedrich, Elsa Bonafonte, Alexander Stephen Oakley, Maciej Zuchowski, Sini Marika Mulari, Anais Lasselin, Marcin Rozanski, Simon Wilbers, Caitlin McMullin, Marzena Zielinska, Janina Shabel, Kadija Begum, Eduardo Lejava, Nivia Marshall, Marisol Cardenas Gallo, Leila Vaziralli, Michal Wowalkowski, Haoyi Wang, Afonso Padras, Efemena Okogba, Daniele Massino Ciprian, Imogen Hamilton, Petry, Sandra Petrasevic, Lesley Strafford, Kazimierz Mazur, Ellie Richold, Peter Ternai, Dariusz Lamecki, Fabio Rodrigues, Sagarvarum Sharma, Tereza Sera, Sandra Jorg Jauernig, Cesar Guerrero, Samuel Sallah, David Sandoval Garcia, Robert Malicin, Miguel Torres, David Febrero lopez, Tero Saavalainen, Daniele Meus, Henry Hryn Acosta, Nathalia Cieslak, Sarah Lever, Agata Cyminska, Edward Bocanegra, Pedro Carvalho, Cerys Bowen, Dimitar Ralev, Karolina Jurga, Mitchell Kardon, Tomasz Kolakowski, Dauron Boltaev, Franco, Alicja Merska, Laura Power, Laure Darcel, Miriam Gontijo, Jose Luis Merino Garcia, Adulai Sabali, Fiona Tang, Tita Cvetkovic, Robert Doka, Cong Fu, Alex Thirlwell, Bing Xia, Lorena Ponte, Mario Rusponi, Marek Micek, Oyeniran Babatunde, Reyes Romero, Ryan Finnegan, Emoke Kilin, Pietro Verde, Tameira McLean, Anna-Cecile Karolina Stepien, Kerry Turley, Guillaume Burguez, Morgen Lorandel, Leonardo Gueli, Brandon Hillman, Miguel Fontalvo, Pedro Miguel Camargo Da Cunha Rego, Ann Jorgensen, Hector Laboure, Andrew Hunt, Manuela Blahova, Ricardo Ditz, Xiaoguang Xu, Alba Vidal, Bruno Massaccesi, Christian Javier Caguana Telenchana, Jay Bernard, Kimberly Morris, Judit Andrassy, Emily Hermon, Aneta Jurkowlaniec, Julia Karimzanova, Bethany Ward, Gavin Williams, Jefferson Freitas, Stefanos Gkouts, Agnieszka Sobolewska, Muhammad Rizwan Shahid, Palacios, Jose Antonio Moreno, Christiane Silva, Bethany Ward, Jana Pajtasova, Inta Lankovska, Ilona Palij, Kirsten Fonzari, Cedric Havard, Nabil Bourassi, Joao Trindade, Fernando Roberto Santo, Combes Guillaume, Rodrigo Menezes De Carvalho, Kristal Maley, Lysette Cook, Kashaka Marcano, Tom Green, Lucy Buckingham, Matthew Alp, Igor Fatou Gaye, Emilie Fournet, Sabine Agoston, Greg Russell, Chloe Martin, Deivid Grigorid, Marta Kowalska, Chiara Scipioni, Gabor Marton, John O'Sullivan, Kher Ying Tey, Joanna Czwakiel, Asad Khan, Rute Christina Coelho da Rocha, Attiya Batool, Paulina Konieczka-Jurkiewicz, Ruth Saunders, S.M Ruhul Amin, Lory Kurosu, May Kovacova, Joe Lawrence, Claire Tully, Edward Bocanegra, Bozena Bobowska, Fernanda Bonifatti, Liliya Georgieva, Corvin Dhali, Daniel Scott, Little, Eric Goncalves, Giuliano Giannini, Mariana Gontijo, Ulpu Inkeri Korhonen, Bozena Bobowska, Sebastien Munch, Sylvain Francescato, Vjaceslavs Sadovskis, Ella Baruch, Luis De Pablo Olivenza, Alice Watson, Olivia Lewis, Carolina Jilderson Svensson, Marina Murinova, Lenka Hajnovicova, Queralt Torrent Llamas, Clement, Samy Dion, Hannah Newman, Loreesa Timms, Louise Mochia, Ben Rider, Jessica Huguet, Elizabeth Okogba, Sarah Young, Tiago Michaelson, Izabela Fabricio Feliciano, Giedre Pociute, Bjorn Tirsen, Jacqueline Tong, Luna Turner, Peter Chytil, Diana Nikolic, Kyle Bellamy, Phoebe Mayer, Filip Tedelund, Anderson Rafa Gesla, Lauren Nightingale, Weronika Wlostowska, Izabela Zeliszczak, Tameira McLean, Jackson Freitas, Thiago Cuadra Garcia, Kassem Yassin, Malgorzata Smiejkowska, Karina Danilo Santos, Rodrigo Muniz, Bhovinder Singh, Marta Adamczyk, Laura Davey, Juliana Rodrigues Mourlan, Rogerio Rius Balestrin, Suzanne Carter, Danilo Cacciola, Luiz Fernando De Custodio, Isabela Antosiewicz, Jessica Dornieden, Richard Holmes, Andre Teixeira, Jozef Depta, Anja Otto, Elizeu De Moura, Joanna Herbert, Aroa Ruiz, Melek Halil, Marius Lakatos, Rodrigues Cleverson Da Silva, Andres Mendoza, Ben Iredale, Ljojcields Hylko, Paulo Rodrigues, Dayane Piffer, Ruby Eyre, Marek Micek, Ben Iredale, Lea Skender, Caroline Linhares, Eleanor Robertson, Bibek Singh, Luiz Alberto Mende De Oliveira, Bernardo Novaes, Lucas Darienco Valenca, Renato Fernandes, Karolina Jurga, Emma Jancauskas, Robson Ribeiro, Roberta Borovskis, Yi Chen Sun, Marco Angelino, Zybowski Jaroslaw, Candy Alderson, Ronaldo Alves, Carolina Pereira, Yago Abella, Luiz Oliveira, Efemena Okogba, Kudratjon Fattakhov, Barry Neale, Rogerio Rius Balestrin, Malgorzata Krogulec, Claudia Cocci Gifroni, Santos, B Tunde, Sandra Svobodova, Joanna Marek, Piotr Maciej Michalski, Renato Fernandes, Linda Abdelhak, Ewa Antonio, Francesco Rossello, Federica Porcu, Lucyjana Gomes de Sousa, Myintzu Zeya, Martina Merickova, Martinez Molero, Sun Liang, Thibaut Strappazon, Wojciech Szczepaniak, Luisa Cruz, Orlan Masilu, Martina Merickova, Laura Pares, Lina Soderland, Tahsin Kucuk, Wilson Fernandes, Ingrida Jurovcikova, Queraat Torrent Lejonqvist, Golam Shohan, Elwira Miechowiecka, Maciej Popiolek, Fedrica Scuito, Roberta Minkute, Martha Szawurska, Lisa McCarthy, Masako Miyazaki, Mara Casolari, Sofia Leddin, Pavel Novacek, Wesley Alves, Vinicius Da Jenny Russell, Renan Amorin, Nicolas Bracamonte, Olga Leddin, Pedro Ribeiro, Wesley Alves, Vinicius Da llamas, Antonio Cardoso, Natalia Balbi Amato, Christopher Swinbourne, Lee Jason Doria, Elisa Santcatterina, Onur Eminogloa, Rikki William Payne, Lauren Griffin, Charlotte Silva, Anthonia Ijegwa Adaji, Stephen Bage, Gemma Lim, Daniel Concannon, Jamie Brenchley, Cheyne Mcmillian, Lucy Harrison, Britton, Sophia Hodson,

Dougie & Claudia Douglas • Kevin Lidlow, Gowrin Motha, Chris Enser • Wellness gurus Wendy Mandy, Wendle Nightingale, Mounir Tourabi, Carole Symons • Dominic Wilhelm

Anita for her beautiful designs and refusal to be phased as deadlines hurtled towards her

Miranda, Jo, Pierre and Jon

Matthew Gordon for being generosity and for being very cool (focus) • Wally Olins, mentor and friend • Spencer, Nick and Gavyn at Active • Roger Siddle for accepting me into the cult • Nick Jackson for keeping me there • Michele Luzi, Mark Gwynne, and Lloyd – may your reward be on earth • We remember Caroline, Brahim and Jay And finally Lenny Kogan (you know who you aren't)

Adam, Sophie, Clemmy, Daisy and Nat Blaker for Sussex love • Kenny and Gabby Logan for friendship (although I don't like the painting with the small heads) • Paul Hayler for early encouragement Mr Hart and Mrs Clarke for very early ' encouragement

Giles and Mark for conceiving the Sustainable Restaurant Association and asking me along for the ride

To my Mum & Dad for magically combining support, warmth, counsel and just as importantly, fun and adventure

Bruno Loubet for giving me my first job and encouraging me to follow a career in food

Roly and Susan neighbourly support

Henry, for being a brilliant business partner

All the ladies in the Bluewater job shop for all their help when we opened Leon Purple • Gemma H • Len Green (Ludgate) • Yenny • Stephen from Fishbowl • Dave & John from Emtone printing • Jo Fontaine from Addison Fowle • Kris Anderson • Iona McDonald from Bluewater Management Team • Yvette from Tibard • Jason Cooper

Dedications:
For my Mother and Father. — HD
For my Mum and Dad. Thank you for so much. And Katie, Natasha and Eleanor. Thank you for everything else. — JV

First publshed in 2010 by Conran Octopus Limited,
a part of Octopus Publishing Group,
Endeavour House, 189 Shaftesbury Avenue, London WC2H 8JY
www.octopusbooks.co.uk

A Hachette UK Company   www.hachette.co.uk

British Library Cataloguing-in-Publication Data.
A catalogue record for this book is available from the British Library.

Publisher: Lorraine Dickey
Managing Editor: Sybella Marlow
Project Manager & Co-cooker: Hattie Deards

Art Director (for Leon): Anita Mangan
Art Director (for Conran Octopus): Jonathan Christie
Illustrations: Anita Mangan (except pages 14–15 Elektra Mandy; 176–77, 202–3 Flora McEvedy;
    165 Madelaine Cooper)
Special Photography: Georgia Glynn Smith

Production Manager: Katherine Hockley

Anita and Stephen, 1970

ISBN: 978 1 84091 556 3
Printed in China

FRESH
TODAY